The Inner Experience

The Inner Experience

Notes on Contemplation

THOMAS MERTON

Edited and with an Introduction by
WILLIAM H. SHANNON

HarperSanFrancisco
A Division of HarperCollins*Publishers*

All biblical quotations in this book are taken from the Douai-Rheims-Challoner version—the only English version approved for Catholics in Merton's day.

HarperCollins books may be purchased for educational, business, or sales promotional use. For information please write: Special Markets Department, HarperCollins Publishers, Inc., 10 East 53rd Street, New York, NY 10022.

HarperCollins Web site: http://www.harpercollins.com

HarperCollins®, 📖®, and HarperSanFrancisco™ are trademarks of HarperCollins Publishers, Inc.

FIRST EDITION

Designed by Kris Tobiassen

Library of Congress Cataloging-in-Publication Data is available upon request.

ISBN 0–06–053928–3 (hardcover)

03 04 05 06 07 ❖/RRD(H) 10 9 8 7 6 5 4 3 2 1

Table of Contents

Introduction

What is contemplation? This question engaged Thomas Merton for most of his adult years. It was also the title of one of his earliest books. *What Is Contemplation?*, written for a student at St. Mary's College, Notre Dame, Indiana, appeared the year in which Merton achieved fame and fortune through the publication of his best-selling autobiography, *The Seven Storey Mountain* (1948). *What Is Contemplation?* would rank quite low on anyone's list of Merton's writings on the contemplative life. There was little about it that was unique. Practically everything in it could be found in almost any work on contemplation written in the first half of the twentieth century. It was not widely advertised and soon yielded place to a better work, *Seeds of Contemplation*, though it must be said that even this work was by no means his best on the subject.

Yet Merton never quite forgot this firstborn of his writings on contemplation. Eleven years after its original publication, in the summer of 1959, he decided to rewrite it. By the end of the summer, he had produced a longer and quite different work, though it still retained within it most of the original. He described it as a finished book, yet he added that it needed some revision. Such a statement raises some obvious questions. When he describes the book as "finished" but needing to be revised, was the revision he had in mind major or minor? Did he actually carry out this revision and, if so, when did he do it?

Evidence from Within the Merton Canon

On July 12, 1959, Merton recorded in his journal: "This week I have been rewriting 'What Is Contemplation?' and of course it has come out three times as long and is a completely different book." A lot of water has gone under the bridge, he tells us, since 1948, when he first wrote the earlier work. In that work his thoughts on contemplation were oversimplified. "How mistaken I was to make contemplation only *part* of a man's life. For a contemplative his whole life is contemplation."[1] Eight days earlier, he had mentioned this project to Sister Thérèse Lentfoehr: "At the moment, guess what, I am rewriting *What Is Contemplation*. It will be a patchy job. But I have been wanting to do it. I may revise other early material, too. It is all very unsatisfactory to me, in fact a lot of it disgusts me." In the earlier work, he tells her, he was much too superficial and too cerebral, concentrating on "a kind of angelism in contemplation." "That was when I was a rip-roaring Trappist, I guess. Now that I am a little less perfect, I seem to have a saner perspective."[2]

His journal entry for July 21, 1959, indicates that he had made a commitment to this project. Already he is expressing some misapprehensions about what he is writing: "Rewriting *What Is Contemplation?*—making too many cracks about 'large monasteries' which are 'like factories.'"[3] Apparently he spent a good bit of the summer working on this revision. Thus at the end of the summer, on September 6, 1959, he is able to say that he has been doing "some rewriting on *Inner Experience* which is now, I think, a respectable book."[4]

It should be noted that the revision he is talking about at this point goes beyond *What Is Contemplation?* It is the revision of a new work that grew out of the revision of that earlier work. He is now revising *The Inner Experience*.

Six days after this entry, on September 12, 1959, writing to Czeslaw Milosz, he speaks about this "respectable book." "I have just been finishing another book, *The Inner Experience*." He summarizes the book's contents for Milosz: "[It offers] a wider deeper view of the same thing, contemplation, with more reference to Oriental ideas. There is to me nothing but this that counts, but everything can enter into it."[5]

There is yet another reference to this newly completed book. On September 29, 1959, he was able to report to Sister Thérèse: "I finished a book this summer called *The Inner Experience* which started out to be a simple revision of *What Is Contemplation* but turned into something new, and just about full length." Although he stated that he had finished the book, he apparently felt that it needed some touching up. He goes on to say: "It has to be revised and has been sitting here on the desk, waiting for revision for some time, but I refuse to work around the house as they are blasting around on all sides with jackhammers and other machines and it is impossible to think. The novices have been making a good share of this noise, trying to put in a couple of new showers in our crowded cellar."[6] Presumably the new showers were installed and the jackhammers and machines eventually stopped their blasting, but neither the Merton *Journals* nor the *Letters* ever indicate that he got around to doing that revision.

In *A Search for Solitude,* the third volume of his *Journals,* under the date of September 29, 1959, the very day he had written to Sister Thérèse, he again expresses a desire to revise it: "My last mss. ('The Inner Experience') lies on the desk untouched. I want to revise it."[7]

On November 19, 1959—a time when he was anticipating a favorable reply from Rome for a transfer to a place of greater solitude—he makes clear that, should this transfer take place, it would probably mean no more writing for him. Yet he hastens to add that there are still three works that need "correcting and proofreading." He lists them: "(A) The Essays—and Xstian Life of Prayer, (B) Existential Communion, and (C) Inner Experience (?)."[8] It is not clear what (A) refers to; (B) was published in 1961 as *The New Man.* The question mark after "Inner Experience" is puzzling. Does it mean that he is no longer sure he wants to rewrite it?

Yet in the fifth volume of the *Journals, Dancing in the Water of Life,* under the date of August 26, 1963, he is still talking about revising it, though there is no proof that he did so at the time. Thus he writes: "Tried to get some of my unfinished work together. With revision of several essays, etc. And revision of *The Inner Experience.*"[9] He "tried" to do this revision, he tells us; but I can find no further reference to "The Inner Experience" in his *Letters* or his *Journals* nor any indication that he actually did revise it. In fact, a curtain is drawn across it, until November 14, 1967, when the

Merton Legacy Trust agreement was drawn up. The Trust agreement would seem to indicate that he had not revised it or at least not to his satisfaction, for, although he gave the Trustees the power to "publish my drafts of books in manuscript form which have not been published," he made two exceptions: "The Inner Experience" and "The School of the Spirit." These were not to be published as books. The Trustees, however, might "permit qualified scholars to quote from said works."[10] In the draft form of his will sent to John Slate,[11] whom Merton had chosen to draw up his will, Merton indicated that "[e]xcerpts [from these two manuscripts] could be published."[12]

This prohibition against publishing "The Inner Experience" strongly suggests that, at the time the Trust document was drawn up (in 1967), he simply had not done the revision he intended; or if he had, he was still not satisfied with it. This evidence supports, beyond any reasonable doubt, my conviction that the four extant drafts of "The Inner Experience" were written in 1959. No revision of the text was made until 1968, when brief (and hardly substantive) corrections and additions were made to draft 4. It is to this 1968 revision that I wish to turn now.

Evidence from Outside the Merton Canon

Is there any indication outside his own writings that would (1) suggest that he did do some revising of the manuscript, (2) tell when he did so, or (3) indicate that, such revisions having been made, Merton was open to the possibility of publishing said manuscript? It is my conviction that Daniel Walsh, Merton's philosophy teacher at Columbia—who had come to Louisville and been ordained a priest in the Louisville diocese—has provided answers to all three of these questions. Walsh did so in a letter he wrote to Father Flavian Burns on May 6, 1972. In this letter he tells Gethsemani's abbot that in 1968, shortly before he left for Asia, Merton paid a surprise visit to him at his office in Bellarmine College. Walsh was about to go across the road (Newburg Road) to give a talk on contemplation to the nuns at the Carmelite monastery. Merton made clear that his visit was a hasty one. He had come to give Walsh a present on the anniversary of his ordination. The date of this visit would have been somewhere near May 14, 1968, since Walsh had been ordained on that date the previous year. His anniversary gift was contained in a manila envelope that he handed to Walsh. Merton told him: "[This] is something I wrote a long time ago, but [I wonder] what the response to it would be if it were published. I had previously decided against it [in the Merton Legacy Trust]. But recently I reread it and made some corrections and additions which you will note in this copy." He suggested that Walsh let the Carmelites read it and find out what they thought about it. "When I get back we can discuss it."

Walsh delivered the manuscript to the Carmelites. They read it in their public reading sessions for a whole year. "They loved it!" Walsh wrote to Abbot Flavian.

The discussion Walsh and Merton were to have on Merton's return never took place, as on December 10, 1968, Merton's voice was forever stilled by his sudden, unexpected, accidental—and much lamented—death in Bangkok, Thailand.

Meanwhile, because of other pressures, Walsh had ceased giving lectures at the Carmelite monastery. When the terrible event of Merton's death became known, he apparently forgot all about the contents of that manila envelope. Then one day when he came to his office, there it was, lying on his desk, returned to him by the Carmelite nuns. He was delighted to find that it contained, as he told Father Flavian, "the original copy of 'The Inner Experience.' It was the corrected version to which Tom had referred." Walsh read it several times and then sent it to Father Flavian with his evaluation: "I am convinced that it is a valuable work and worthy of publication as a book."[13]

This letter of Daniel Walsh to Father Flavian does answer the three questions posed above. Merton spoke to Walsh about "something I wrote a long time ago." That "long time ago" would be the summer of 1959. He did revise this work, which he had written in 1959. When did he do it? He told Walsh that recently he had made "some corrections and additions." The time he visited Walsh was shortly before he left for Asia. This would strongly indicate that such recent "corrections and additions" had been made in 1968 (and therefore subsequent to the signing of the Trust agreement). Finally, it seems clear that, once the corrections and additions had been made, he had a change of heart about the possible publication of "The Inner Experience." In his letter to Abbot Flavian, Walsh affirmed: "There is no doubt in my mind that [because of the additional work done on the text?] Tom's thinking about the publication of the work had changed since the writing of the Trust." Father Flavian agreed with Walsh and was in favor of having this work published. John Ford, the lawyer for the Merton Trust, gave the legal judgment that oral evidence (Walsh's testimony) could not set aside the written will. This seemed to settle the matter. "The Inner Experience" could not be published.

In 1981 I published a book called *Thomas Merton's Dark Path,*[14] which gave a summary of the contents of "The Inner Experience" and a selection of texts that amounted to about 20 percent of the manuscript. This was permitted by the Trust because Merton had stipulated that, although it should not be published as a book, qualified scholars could quote from it.

In 1983 *Cistercian Studies Quarterly* was given permission to publish major portions of "The Inner Experience" serially. This it did in the eight issues of 1983 and 1984. These were then made available in eight reprints. To make these reprints more easily available, the editor decided to have the eight bound in two booklets, four reprints in each. Without realizing it, *Cistercian Studies,* by putting these reprints into booklets, had unwittingly published *The Inner Experience.* A call to the Library of Congress made by one of the Trustees confirmed the fact that it was now listed as a published book. Then in 1992, Lawrence S. Cunningham included the first of these two booklets in his book of Merton texts entitled *Thomas Merton, Spiritual Master: The Essential Writings.*[15]

In the light of all this information about portions of *The Inner Experience* having appeared in various forms, the Merton Trust made the decision that the time had come to have *The Inner Experience* published in a form that would do justice to Merton and to the manuscript he wrote. This meant a publication that would offer (1) a careful editing of the text, (2) a clarification of how it got to be as it is, (3) a positioning of it in its proper historical place in the Merton corpus, and (4) an indication of its importance in that corpus. These goals represent the intent of this present edition of *The Inner Experience.*

Editing the Text

The editing of *The Inner Experience* posed its own unique problem. The typescript exists in four drafts[16] that are in the possession of the Thomas Merton Center at Bellarmine University, but unfortunately all of these drafts are copies, not original texts; moreover, they are undated. It was my good fortune to be able to locate and use the original text that Merton gave to Daniel Walsh in 1968. It contains in handwritten form the "corrections and additions" Merton told Walsh that he had made recently (that is, just before he left for Asia). In all, these corrections and additions amount to about 450 words. Of these words, a passage of 125 is inserted early in the text. The rest of the additions and corrections amount to a sentence, a phrase, or a word or two. Mostly they are clarifications adding little that is new to the text. A manuscript page is about 430 words. Hence all the corrections and additions taken together amount to little more than one page of a 151-page typescript.

This draft, because it has the final corrections and additions Merton wanted to make, I have called draft 4, though Merton did not give it any designation. Draft 3 (which is so designated in the copy at Bellarmine University) is identical to draft 4, except that it lacks the corrections and additions and has a slightly different pagination.

Dating the Text

My conclusion about the dating of *The Inner Experience* is the following. From the evidence cited above it seems clear that during the summer of 1959 four drafts were written. These were completed by sometime in September 1959. In spite of his desire to revise the work, he never got to do such revision until 1968, just before he left for Asia. The "corrections and additions" he made at that time were not substantive. *The Inner Experience,* therefore, remains by and large a work of 1959.

The draft called "draft 1" could hardly qualify as the "finished book" described to Sister Thérèse and Milosz: it is full of inserts, some handwritten, some typed, some single-spaced. It would be well near impossible to find a coherent way of reading it.[17]

Draft 4 has everything in it that one will find in the other three; it also has the "corrections and additions" of 1968. It is my conviction that when Merton wrote (to Sister Thérèse and to Milosz) about having finished a book, he was talking about draft 4 (without the corrections and additions) or draft 3, which is basically the same. This is the text he kept saying he must revise, but there is no evidence that he did so until 1968. Why 1968? Because it was sometime that summer that he told Walsh he had recently made "corrections and additions" to a book that he had written a long time ago.

It is this text of 1959 with the additions and corrections of 1968 that is being used in this present work.

The Importance of 'The Inner Experience' in the Merton Corpus

The Inner Experience has an important place in the Merton corpus and in his writings about contemplation. This importance is more readily appreciated when one realizes that, except for the relatively few corrections and additions of 1968, the work belongs to the year 1959.[18] Written at that time, it may be seen as a "bridge" between the early and later Merton. In this work he makes clear that contemplation is not a compartment of life, but rather the way to integrate one's life into a single whole. The distinction between the false self and the true self that he touched on briefly in Seeds of Contemplation[19] receives fuller expression and prepares the way for the striking description of that distinction in the last part of "Notes for a Philosophy of Solitude" (1960)[20] and its lyrical expression in New Seeds of Contemplation (1962). Further, we see here for the first time Merton forging a link with Eastern religious thought,[21] in striking contrast to his facile dismissal of oriental religions in Seeds of Contemplation.[22] Concurrent with this contact with the East was his attraction to existential thought (references to various existential writers are cited with appreciation).[23] One discovers also a shift away from the dualism that marred his earlier works. There are clear indications of his "return to the world" with a sense of compassion for people that clearly marks a departure from the excessive "world-denying position" of some of the earlier writings. He understands more positively the role of the lay vocation in the Church, though he is perhaps a bit naïve in his suggestions about the directions that vocation might take.[24]

Merton's letter of September 12, 1959, to Czeslaw Milosz, cited above, is a helpful summary of the contents of *The Inner Experience:* "I have just been finishing another book, *The Inner Experience*—a wider deeper view of the same thing, contemplation, with more reference to Oriental ideas. There is to me nothing but this that counts, but everything can enter into it." Note four points: (1) *The Inner Experience* is a book about contemplation. (2) Merton plans to offer a more comprehensive view of that subject ("wider deeper view"). (3) He will show how Christian contemplation relates to Eastern religious thought. (4) Contemplation relates to the whole of human life and integrates that life into a single whole ("everything can enter into it"). The points made in this quotation may serve as a useful guide for readers as they make their way through the pages of this book.

It is my conviction that the contents of this work hang together better than some commentators on the text have been inclined to think.[25] It has been declared "incomplete" or "unfinished." Michael Casey sees it as "assembled in an atmosphere of deliberate disarray."[26] It is true that the chapter numbering (or lack of numbering) is a bit puzzling, though in the end it works out all right. It is equally true that each of the chapters could stand alone and be read for its own sake. (But is this not true of other books of Merton's, e.g., *New Seeds of Contemplation?*) Yet there is a unity discoverable among these separate chapters—a unity that can be seen in Merton's description of the book in his letter to Milosz.

It is helpful also to look at the subtitle Merton gave to this work: "Notes on Contemplation." "Notes" suggests that his intent was not a full-blown discussion of contemplation, but a setting forth of elements that must be included in any such discussion. In this respect, "Notes on Contemplation" is not unlike his "Notes for a Philosophy of Solitude," which would appear a year later as a chapter in *Disputed Questions* (1960). Just as it would be wrong to approach that essay seeking in it a complete treatment of a philosophy of solitude, so it would be equally mistaken to look to *The Inner Experience* for a comprehensive treatise on contemplation. Merton, in my opinion, did not intend, nor did he even believe in the possibility of, a once-and-for-all treatment of contemplation that would be complete and definitive.

A Typographical Note

Since *The Inner Experience* was begun as a revision of *What Is Contemplation?* and since Merton has incorporated most of that earlier work into his final text, I have used a distinctively different type font for identifying passages from *What Is Contemplation?* Moreover, I have put in italics the changes that Merton made with his "corrections and additions" of 1968. In the notes for each chapter I have indicated what was corrected or added. In most cases, it was simply a matter of choosing more appropriate words or phrases. In one place a paragraph has been added and in a few other cases an entire sentence. As indicated earlier, all the changes taken together amount to a little more than a single manuscript page. Finally, words, phrases, or sentences that Merton italicized have no note number.

Appendices

Appendix A gives the various texts from the Merton *Journals* and *Letters* in which references are made to *The Inner Experience*. Appendix B is a table intended for those readers who may have a scholarly interest in understanding the relationships of the various drafts of *The Inner Experience* to one another.

Acknowledgments

I want to express my gratitude to Diane Addante for the initial typing of the manuscript and to Brother Patrick Hart and Dr. Christine Bochen for their encouragement and helpful suggestions. In a special way I would like to express my appreciation to the Trustees of the Merton Legacy Trust, Anne McCormick, Robert Giroux, and Thomasine O'Callaghan, for entrusting to me the happy task of preparing *The Inner Experience* for publication.

—WILLIAM H. SHANNON

[O N E]

A Preliminary Warning

Man in our day, menaced on all sides with ruin, is at the same time beset with illusory promises of happiness. Both threat and promise often come from the same political source. Both hell and heaven have become, so [they say], immediate possibilities here on earth. It is true that the emotional hell and the heaven which each one of us carries about within him tend to become more and more public and common property. And as time goes on it seems evident that what we have to share seems to be not so much one another's heaven as one another's hell.

For the desire which we cherish, in the secrecy of our soul, as our "heaven" *sometimes*[1] turns, when offered as a solution to common problems, into everybody's hell. This is one of the curious features of twentieth-century civilization, and of its discontents.

Into the midst of this moral and emotional chaos, popular psychologists and religious teachers, men of pathetic optimism and good will, have rushed forward hopefully to announce their message of comfort. Seldom concerned with the afterlife, whether good or evil, as befits men of our time, they want to set things right for us here and now. They want us, at all costs, to be inspired, uplifted. They fret over our distressing tendencies to see the dark side of modern life, because they are able to imagine that it has a light side somewhere. Have we not, after all, made the most remarkable progress? Is the standard of living not rising every day, and is not our lot becoming always better and better, so that soon we will have to work less and less in order to enjoy more and more? With a dash of psychological self-help and a decent minimum of religious conformity, we can adjust ourselves to the emptiness of lives that are so blissfully devoid of struggle, sacrifice, or effort. These willing counselors want to revive our confidence in all the gestures of bourgeois good feeling which will magically turn pain into pleasure and sorrow into joy because God is in His heaven and all's right with the world.

At such time it would be singularly unfeeling as well as dishonest for me to suggest that peace, joy, and happiness are easily found along that most arid stretch of man's spiritual pilgrimage: the life of contemplation. More often than not, the way of contemplation is not even a way, and if one follows it, what he finds is nothing. Later on in these pages we hope to justify the apparent fruitlessness of the quest. But at present it is *important*[2] to make clear that this book has no intention of solving anybody's problems, or of offering anybody an easy way out of his difficulties. At best it may help to bring a little reassurance to those whose difficulties are characteristically spiritual and contemplative—which means that they are barely possible to formulate at all. One of the strange laws of the contemplative life is that in it you do not sit down and solve problems: you bear with them until they somehow solve themselves. Or until life itself solves them for you. Usually the solution consists in a discovery that they only existed insofar as they were inseparably connected with your own illusory exterior self. The solution of most such problems comes with the dissolution of this false self. And consequently another law of the contemplative life is that if you enter it with the set purpose of seeking contemplation, or worse still, happiness, you will find neither. For neither can be found unless it is first in some sense renounced. And again, this means renouncing the illusory self that seeks to be "happy" and to find "fulfillment" (whatever that may mean) in contemplation. For the contemplative and spiritual self, the dormant, mysterious, and hidden self that is always effaced by the activity of our exterior self does not seek fulfillment. It is content to *be,* and in its being it is fulfilled, because its being is rooted in God.

If, then, you are intent on "becoming a contemplative" you will probably waste your time and do yourself considerable harm by reading this book. But if in some sense you are already a contemplative (whether you know it or not makes little difference), you will perhaps not only read the book with a kind of obscure awareness that it is meant for you, but you may even find yourself having to read the thing whether *it fits in with your plans*[3] or not. In that event, just read it. Do not watch for the results, for they will already have been produced long before you will be capable of seeing them. And pray for me, because from now on we are, in some strange way, good friends.

The purpose of this opening is not simply to *punish*[4] the reader or deliberately to discourage him, but to make clear that this book in no sense aspires to be classified as "inspirational." That is to say, it does not aim at making the reader feel good about certain spiritual opportunities which it claims, at the same time, to open up to him. Nor does it pretend to remind anyone of a duty he has failed to perform or attempt to show him how to perform it better. It does not claim to *deliver*[5] a new and original message that has been hitherto ignored and which will restore true perspectives falsified by the short-sightedness of "other spiritual writers." And, finally, it contains no meretricious promise that one can become a kind of superior being by enrolling himself in an esoteric elite of so-called contemplatives. It does not prescribe any new devout attitudes. It does not encourage a ceremonious and self-righteous withdrawal from everyday reality. It is not exclusively in favor of passivity and inertia. It prescribes no special psychophysical techniques (although these can certainly have their rightful place in the spiritual life).

The worst thing that can happen to a man who is already divided up into a dozen different compartments is to seal off yet another compartment and tell him that this one is more important than all the others, and that he must henceforth exercise a special care in keeping it separate from them. That is what tends to happen when contemplation is unwisely thrust without warning upon the bewilderment and distraction of Western man. *The Eastern traditions have the advantage of disposing man more naturally for contemplation.*[6]

The first thing that you have to do, before you even start thinking about such a thing as contemplation, is to try to recover your basic natural unity, to *reintegrate*[7] your compartmentalized being into a coordinated and simple whole and learn to live as a unified *human person*.[8] This means that you have to bring back together the fragments of your distracted existence so that when you say "I," there is really someone present to support the pronoun you have uttered.

Reflect, sometimes, on the disquieting fact that most of your statements of opinions, tastes, deeds, desires, hopes, and fears are statements about someone who is not really present. When you say "I think," it is often not you who think, but "they"—it is the anonymous authority of the collectivity speaking through your mask. When you say "I want," you are sometimes simply making an automatic gesture of accepting, paying for, what has been forced upon you. That is to say, you reach out for what you have been made to want.

Who is this "I" that you imagine yourself to be? An easy and pragmatic branch of psychological thought will tell you that if you can hook up your pronoun with your proper name and declare that you are the bearer of that name, you know who you are. You are "aware of yourself as a person." Perhaps there is a beginning of truth in this: it is better to describe yourself with a name that is yours alone than with a noun that applies to a whole species. For then you are evidently aware of yourself as an individual *subject*,[9] and not just as *an object*,[10] or as a nameless unit in a multitude. It is true that for modern man even to be able to call himself by his own proper name is an achievement that evokes wonder both in himself and in others. But this is only a beginning, and a beginning that primitive man would perhaps have been able to laugh at. For when a person appears to know his own name, it is still no guarantee that he is aware of the name as representing a real person. On the contrary, it may be the name of a fictitious character occupied in very active self-impersonation in the world of business, of politics, of scholarship, or of religion.

This, however, is not the "I" who can stand in the presence of God and be aware of Him as a "Thou." For this "I" there is perhaps no clear "Thou" at all. Perhaps even other people are merely extensions of the "I," reflections of it, modifications of it, aspects of it. Perhaps for this "I" there is no clear distinction between itself and other objects: it may find itself immersed in the world of objects and to have lost its own subjectivity, even though it may be very conscious and even aggressively definite in saying "I."

If such an "I" one day hears about "contemplation," he will perhaps set himself to "become a contemplative." That is, he will wish to admire, in himself, something called contemplation. And in order to see it, he will reflect on his alienated self. He will make contemplative faces at himself like a child in front of a mirror. He will cultivate the contemplative look that seems appropriate to him and that he likes to see in himself. And the fact that his busy narcissism is turned within and feeds upon itself in stillness and secret love will make him believe that *his experience of himself is an experience of God.*[11]

But the exterior "I," the "I" of projects, of temporal finalities, the "I" that manipulates objects in order to take possession of them, is alien from the hidden, interior "I" who has no projects and seeks to accomplish nothing, even contemplation. He seeks only to be, and to move (for he is dynamic) according to the secret laws of Being itself and according to the promptings of a Superior Freedom (that is, of God), rather than to plan and to achieve according to his own desires.

It will be ironical, indeed, if the exterior self seizes upon something within himself and slyly manipulates it as if to take possession of some inner contemplative secret, imagining that this manipulation can somehow lead to the emergence of an inner self. The inner self is precisely that self which cannot be tricked or manipulated by anyone, even by the devil. He is like a very shy wild animal that never appears at all whenever an alien presence is at hand, and comes out only when all is perfectly *peaceful,*[12] in silence, when he is untroubled and alone. He cannot be lured by anyone or anything, because he responds to no lure except that of the divine freedom.

Sad is the case of that exterior self that imagines himself contemplative, and seeks to achieve contemplation as the fruit of planned effort and of spiritual ambition. He will assume varied attitudes, meditate on the inner significance of his own postures, and try to fabricate for himself a contemplative identity: and all the while there is nobody there. There is only an illusory, fictional "I" which seeks itself, struggles to create itself out of nothing, maintained in being by its own compulsion and the prisoner of his private illusion.

The call to contemplation is not, and cannot, be addressed to such an "I."

[T W O]

The Awakening
of the Inner Self

From what has been said, it is clear that there is and can be no special planned technique for discovering and awakening one's inner self, because the inner self is, first of all, a spontaneity that is nothing if not free. Therefore there is no use in trying to start with a definition of the inner self, and then deducing from its essential properties some appropriate and infallible means of submitting it to control—as if the essence could give us some clue to that which is vulnerable in it, something we can lay hold of in order to gain power over it. Such an idea would imply a complete misapprehension of the *existential*[1] reality we are talking about. The inner self is not a part of our being, like a motor in a car. It is our entire substantial reality itself, on its highest and most personal and most existential level. It is like life, and it is life: it is our spiritual life when it is most alive. It is the life by which everything else in us lives and moves. It is in and through and beyond everything that we are. If it is awakened, it communicates a new life to the intelligence in which it lives, so that it becomes a living awareness of itself: and this awareness is not so much something that we ourselves have, as something that we are. It is a new and indefinable quality of our living being.

The inner self is as secret as God and, like Him, it evades every concept that tries to seize hold of it with full possession. It is a life that cannot be held and studied as object, because it is not "a thing." It is not reached and coaxed forth from hiding by any process under the sun, including meditation. All that we can do with any spiritual discipline is produce within ourselves something of the silence, the humility, the detachment, the purity of heart, and the indifference which are required if the inner self is to make some shy, unpredictable manifestation of *his*[2] presence.

At the same time, however, every deeply spiritual experience, whether religious, moral, or even artistic, tends to have in it something of the presence of the interior self. Only from the inner self does any spiritual experience gain depth, reality, and a certain incommunicability. But the depth of ordinary spiritual experience only gives us a derivative sense of the inner self. It reminds us of the forgotten levels of interiority in our spiritual nature, and of our helplessness to explore them.

Nevertheless, a certain cultural and spiritual atmosphere favors the secret and spontaneous development of the inner self. The ancient cultural traditions, both of the East and of the West, having a religious and sapiential nature, favored the interior life, indeed transmitted certain common materials in the form of archetypal symbols, liturgical notes, art, poetry, philosophy, and myth, which nourished the inner self from childhood to maturity. In such a cultural setting no one needs to be self-conscious about his interior life, and subjectivity does not run the risk of being deviated into morbidity and excess. Unfortunately such a cultural setting no longer exists in the West or is no longer common property. It is something that has to be laboriously recovered by an educated and enlightened minority.[3]

An Example from Zen

Although this book is mainly concerned with Christian mysticism, we might profitably pause to consider an example of inner awakening taken from an oriental text. It is a cryptic and telling instance of interior self-realization, and the elements in the experience are so clearly set out that they provide an almost "clinically perfect" test case in the natural order. This is an account of *satori*, a spiritual enlightenment, a bursting open of the inner core of the spirit to reveal the inmost self. This takes place in the peace of what we might ordinarily call contemplation, but it breaks through suddenly and by surprise, beyond the level of quiet contemplative absorption, showing that mere interior peace does not suffice to bring us in contact with our deepest liberty.

The thing that is most helpful about this example is that it makes no claims whatever to be supernatural or mystical. *Zen is, in a sense, antimystical.*[4] Hence it permits us to observe the *natural* working of the inner self. In fact, the chief spokesman for Zen today, D. T. Suzuki, goes to some pains to contrast this spiritual event with Christian mystical experience, laying stress on its "natural" character as a "purely psychological" phenomenon. Hence no one will be offended if we presume to examine this as a psychological case, showing the workings of the inner self presumably without any influence of mystical grace. [*Whether or not such an experience is actually possible without grace, and on a purely natural level, and whether it might be possible to contradict Suzuki and to call it mystical might form the subject of a provocative study. At the moment, for the sake of convenience, I am taking Suzuki's word and accepting the example exactly as he presents it and on his own terms, as a purely natural, empirical fact.*][5]

Satori, which is the very heart and essence of Zen, is a revolutionary spiritual experience in which, after prolonged purification and trial, and of course after determined spiritual discipline, the monk experiences a kind of inner explosion that blasts his false exterior self to pieces and leaves nothing but "his original face," his "original self before you were born," [*or, more technically, his "Buddha nature." Whatever you want to call this real self*—the purusha *(spirit) of Hindu philosophy, the* tathagatha, *or "suchness," of Zen*—*it is that inner "I" that we are discussing at present.*][6]

This was the experience of a Chinese official of the Sung dynasty[7] who was a lay disciple of one of the Zen masters. Chao-pien, the official, was sitting quietly in his office, at leisure, with his mind at rest in what we would call simple contemplative prayer. According to the Zen theory, he had reached that point of inner maturity where the secret pressure of the inner self was ready to break unexpectedly forth and revolutionize his whole being in *satori.* When one reaches such a point, say the Zen masters, any fortuitous sound, word, or happening is likely to set off the explosion of "enlightenment" which consists in large part in the sudden, definitive integral realization of the nothingness of the exterior self and, consequently, the liberation of the real self, the inner "I." *Yet these are Western terms. The real self, in Zen language, is beyond the division between self and not-self.*[8] Chao-pien was sitting there at peace when he heard a clap of thunder, and the "mind doors burst open," in the depths of his silent being, to reveal his "original self," *or "suchness."*[9] The whole incident is summarized, according to Chinese custom, in a four-line poem, and it has rightly become immortal:

> *Devoid of thought, I sat quietly by the desk in my official room,*
> *With my fountain-mind undisturbed, as serene as water;*
> *A sudden crash of thunder, the mind doors burst open,*
> *And lo, there sits the old man in all his homeliness.*[10]

As an example of spiritual experience this is likely to perplex and even to scandalize those who expect all such things to be quite otherworldly and ethereal. But that is precisely what makes it incomparable for our purpose. Suzuki, incidentally, with his usual love of irony, capitalizes on the dry, unsentimental humor of the experience to contrast it with the more affective flights of amorous mysticism with which we are familiar in the West.[11] Unfortunately, the lack of erotic or affective notes does not set *this experience*[12] apart as distinctly "oriental" at all. In all spiritualities there is a contrast between the *affective or*[13] devotional (*bhakti*) and the intellectual, anoetic type of experience (*raja yoga*). This story may have a distinctively Chinese flavor, but anyone familiar with *The Cloud of Unknowing* and other documents of Western apophatic mysticism will be perfectly at home with it.

And so Chao-pien finds himself with his false self blown to smithereens, and with the fragments carried away as though by a sudden, happy cyclone. There sits Chao-pien himself, the same and yet utterly different, for it is the eternal Chao-pien, one with *no familiar name,*[14] at once humble and mighty, terrible and funny, and utterly beyond description or comparison because he is *beyond yes and no, subject and object, self and not-self.*[15] It is *like*[16] the wonderful, devastating, and unutterable awe of humble joy with which a *Christian*[17] realizes: "I and the Lord are One," and when, if one tries to explain this oneness in any way possible to human speech—for instance, as the merging of two entities—one must always qualify: "No, not like that, not like that." That is why, of course, Suzuki wants to make quite plain that nothing is really said in this event about union with "Another." Well, all right. Let us assume it is perfectly natural . . . In any case the event is full of significant elements and throws much light on what I have been trying to explain.

First of all, even before his *satori* Chao-pien is in a condition of tranquil recollection. [*He is devoid of "thought." He has entered into the "cloud of unknowing," in which the mind is "pure" but by no means blank, passive, or inactive. For this emptiness is also a kind of fullness, and this stillness is not dead or inert. It is filled with infinite possibilities and stands poised in expectation of their fulfillment, with no comprehension of what that fulfillment may be and no desire for it to take any special preconceived form or direction. This is described as a "fountain-mind," which suggests, at least to me, that it is capable of receiving, and perhaps is actually receiving, from it knows not where and with no evidence of psychological effort, something that it knows not and about which it is unconcerned.*][18]

This placid unknowing is not yet *awareness of*[19] the true inner self. But it is a natural climate in which the spiritual self may yield up its secret identity. Suddenly there is a clap of thunder and the "doors" of the *inner*[20] consciousness fly open. The clap of thunder is just startling enough to create a sudden awareness, a self-realization in which the false, exterior self is caught in all its naked nothingness and immediately dispelled as an illusion. Not only does it vanish, but it is seen never to have been there at all—a pure fiction, a mere shadow of passionate attachment and of self-deception. Instead, the real self stands revealed in all his reality. The term "old man" must of course not be given Pauline connotations. In St. Paul's language this would, on the contrary, be the "new man." [*Why "old"? Because of the Buddhist belief that the true self has existed from all eternity in the uncreated Absolute and is itself "uncreated." Such a self is ever old and ever new because it is beyond old and new. It lives in eternity.*][21]

But why is this self described as "homely"? In some cases of *satori*, the inner self appears as wonderful or even terrifying, like a roaring lion with a golden mane. Such cases might find analogues in the poetry of William Blake. But here Chao-pien is happy with his "old man in all his homeliness" perhaps because he is thoroughly relieved to discover that the real self is utterly simple, humble, poor, and unassuming. The inner self is not an *ideal* self, especially not an imaginary, perfect creature fabricated to measure up to our compulsive need for greatness, heroism, and infallibility. On the contrary, the real "I" is just simply ourself and nothing more. Nothing more, nothing less. Our self as we are in the eyes of God, to use Christian terms. Our self in all our uniqueness, dignity, littleness, and ineffable greatness: the greatness we have received from God our Father and that we share with Him because He is our Father and "In Him we live and move and have our being" (Acts 17:28).

The laconic little poem, then, expresses the full sense of liberation experienced by one who recognizes, with immense relief, that he is not his false self after all, and that he has all along been nothing else but his real and "homely" self, and nothing more, without glory, without self-aggrandizement, without self-righteousness, and without self-concern.

The Christian Approach

This discovery of the inner self plays a familiar part in Christian mysticism. But there is a significant difference, which is clearly brought out by St. Augustine. In Zen there seems to be no effort to get *beyond* the inner self. In Christianity the inner self is simply a stepping stone to an awareness of God. Man is the image of God, and his inner self is a kind of mirror in which God not only sees Himself, but reveals Himself to the "mirror" in which He is reflected. Thus, through the dark, transparent mystery of our own inner being we can, as it were, see God "through a glass." All this is of course pure metaphor. It is a way of saying that our being somehow communicates directly with the Being of God, Who is "in us." If we enter into ourselves, find our true self, and then pass "beyond" the inner "I," we sail forth into the immense darkness in which we confront the "I AM" of the Almighty.

The Zen writers might perhaps contend that they were interested exclusively in what is actually "given" in their experience, and that Christianity is superadding a theological interpretation and extrapolation on top of the experience itself. But here we come upon one of the distinctive features of

Christian, Jewish, and Islamic mysticisms. For us, there is an infinite metaphysical gulf between the being of God and the being of the soul, between the "I" of the Almighty and our own inner "I." Yet paradoxically our inmost "I" exists in God and God dwells in it. But it is nevertheless necessary to distinguish between the experience of one's own inmost being and the awareness that God has revealed Himself to us in and through our inner self. We must know that the mirror is distinct from the image reflected in it. The difference rests on theological *faith*.

Our awareness of our inner self can at least theoretically be the fruit of a purely natural and psychological purification. Our awareness of God is a supernatural participation in the light by which He reveals Himself interiorly as dwelling in our inmost self. Hence the Christian mystical experience is not only an awareness of the inner self, but also, by a supernatural intensification of faith, it is an experiential grasp of God as present within our inner self. In the interests of brevity, let us proceed without further explanation to a few classical texts, first from St. Augustine:

Is God, then, anything of the same nature as the soul? This mind of ours seeks to find something that is God. It seeks to find a Truth not subject to change, a Substance not capable of failing. The mind itself is not of this nature: it is capable of progress and decay, of knowledge and of ignorance, of remembering or forgetting. That mutability is not incident to God.

Having therefore sought to find my God in visible and corporeal things, and found Him not; having sought to find His substance in myself and found Him not, I perceive my God to be something higher than my soul. Therefore that I might attain to Him I thought on these things and poured out my soul above myself. When would my soul attain to that object of its search, which is "above my soul," if my soul were not to pour itself out above itself? For were it to rest in itself, it would not see anything else beyond itself, would not, for all that, see God. . . . I have poured forth my soul above myself and there remains no longer any being for me to attain to save my God. . . . His dwelling place is above my soul; from thence He beholds me, from thence He governs me and provides for me; from thence He appeals to me, calls me and directs me; leads me in the way and to the end of my way.
(*Enarratio in Psalm 41*)

* * *

And being by them (that is, by the Platonists) admonished to return to
myself, I entered even to my inmost self, Thou being my guide. I entered
and beheld with the eye of the soul, above the same eye of my soul, above
my mind, the Light unchangeable . . . And Thou didst beat back the weakness of my sight, streaming forth Thy beams of light upon me most strongly,
and I trembled with love and awe. (*Confessions* vii, 16; translations taken from
Dom Cuthbert Butler, *Western Mysticism,* pp. 22, 31)

The intellectual and Platonizing speculations of St. Augustine put us in
a very different experiential climate from what we have just discussed in
Zen, and it is therefore not easy to say where to place the "inmost self" of
which Augustine speaks. There is always a possibility that what an Eastern
mystic describes as Self is what the Western mystic will describe as God,
because we shall see presently that the mystical union between the soul
and God renders them in some sense "undivided" (though metaphysically
distinct) in spiritual experience. And the fact that the Eastern mystic, not
conditioned by centuries of theological debate, may not be inclined to
reflect on the fine points of metaphysical distinction does not necessarily
mean that he has not experienced the presence of God when he speaks of
knowing the Inmost Self.

Let us turn to some texts of the Rhenish Dominican mystic John
Tauler.[22] For him, the inner self, the inmost "I," is the "ground" or "center"
or "apex" of the soul. Trained in the tradition of Augustine, Tauler is, however, more concrete and less speculative than his masters, except Eckhart,[23]
whose resemblances to oriental mysticism are being fully studied today. Here
is Tauler in a passage that reminds [one] of Chao-pien's "fountain-mind":

Now man with all his faculties and also with his soul recollects himself and
enters into the temple (his inner self) in which, in all truth, he finds God
dwelling and at work. Man then comes to experience God not after the
fashion of the senses and of reason, or like something that one understands
or reads . . . but he tastes Him, and enjoys Him like something that springs
up from the "ground" of the soul as from its own source, or from a fountain,
without having been brought there, for a fountain is better than a cistern,

the water of cisterns gets stale and evaporates, but the spring flows, bursts out, swells: it is true, not borrowed. It is sweet. *(Sermon for the Thursday before Palm Sunday)*

In another passage, Tauler speaks of the deep contact between the "ground" of the soul and God, following an interior upheaval and purification produced mystically by the action of God. While in the previous quotation there was a resemblance to the fountain in the Chinese text, here is a clap of "mystical thunder":

After this, one should open the ground of the soul and the deep will to the sublimity of the glorious Godhead, and look upon Him with great and humble fear and denial of oneself. He who in this fashion casts down before God his shadowy and unhappy ignorance then begins to understand the words of Job, who said: The spirit passed before me. From this passage of the Spirit is born a great tumult in the soul. And the more this passage has been clear, true, unmixed with natural impressions, all the more rapid, strong, prompt, true and pure will be the work which takes place in the soul, the thrust which overturns it; clearer also will be the knowledge that man has stopped on the path to perfection. The Lord then comes like a flash of lightning; he fills the ground of the soul with light and wills to establish Himself there as the Master Workman. As soon as one is conscious of the presence of the Master, one must, in all passivity, abandon the work to Him. (*Second Sermon for the Exaltation of the Holy Cross, #5*)

It is obvious that all metaphors are unsatisfactory in this delicate matter. Tauler's "ground" is *effective*[24] insofar as it conveys the idea of that which is most fundamental in our being, as the rock on which everything else is built as on a foundation. But this is a spiritual "rock" which suddenly ceases to be a rock and becomes transparent and full of light: for it has at the same time the qualities of hardness and solidity, and yet also transparency and penetrability. It is as if it were both rock and air, earth and atmosphere. It can suddenly come alive from within, as with a flash of lightning! Of course the idea of ground also suggests soil from which things grow. The language of mystics, in short, is always poetic and claims plenty of license for paradox in dealing freely with symbols, sweeping them far outside the limits of their own capacity to convey a meaning.

According to the Christian mystical tradition, one cannot find one's inner center and know God there as long as one is involved in the preoccupations and desires of the outward self. Tauler, in the lines just quoted, suggests that even the depths of the soul can be troubled with what he calls "natural impressions," which are sense-bound and involved in temporal conflict. Penetration into the depths of our being is, then, a matter of liberation from the ordinary flow of conscious and half-conscious sense impressions, but also and more definitely from the unconscious drives and the clamoring of inordinate passion. Freedom to enter the inner sanctuary of our being is denied to those who are held back by dependence on self-gratification and sense satisfaction, whether it be a matter of pleasure seeking, love of comfort, or proneness to anger, self-assertion, pride, vanity, greed, and all the rest.

St. John of the Cross[25] seems to include all this freedom and more still under the one heading of "faith." Faith is indeed the "dark night" in which we meet God, according to St. John of the Cross. "This dark and loving knowledge, which is faith, serves as a means of divine union in this life, even as in the next life the light of glory serves as an intermediary to the clear knowledge of God" (*Ascent of Mount Carmel* II, xxiv, 4). Faith in this sense is more than the assent to dogmatic truths proposed for belief by "the authority of God revealing." It is a personal and direct acceptance of God Himself, a "receiving" of the Light of Christ in the soul, and a consequent beginning or renewal of spiritual life. But an essential element in this reception of the "light" of Christ is the *rejection* of every other "light" that can appeal to sense, passion, imagination, or intellect.

Faith, for St. John, is simultaneously a turning to God and a turning away from God's creatures—a blacking out of the visible in order to see the invisible. The two ideas are inseparable for him, and on their inseparability depend his inexorable logic and his pitiless asceticism. But it is important to remember that the mere blacking out of sensible things is not faith, and will not serve as a means to bring faith into existence. It is the other way round. Faith is a light of such supreme brilliance that it dazzles the mind and darkens all its vision of other realities: but in the end, when we become used to the new light, we gain a new vision of all reality trans-figured and elevated in the light itself. As the saint remarks:

> This excessive light of faith which is given to the soul is thick darkness, for it overwhelms that which is great and does away with that which is little, even as the light of the sun overwhelms all other lights whatsoever, so that when it shines and disables our vision they appear to be no lights at all. (*Ascent of Mount Carmel,* ii, iii, 1)

This, too, is of course metaphor. The "blindness" to exterior things is a question of interpretation and evaluation. The contemplative does not cease to *know* external objects. But he ceases to be *guided* by them. He ceases to depend on them. He ceases to treat them as ultimate. He evaluates them in a new way, in which they are no longer objects of desire or fear, but remain neutral and, as it were, empty until such time as they too become filled with the light of God.

During the "dark night" of faith, one must let himself be guided to reality not by visible and tangible things, not by the evidence of sense or the understanding of reason, not by concepts charged with natural hope, or joy, or fear, or desire, or grief, but by "dark faith" that transcends all desire and seeks no human and earthly satisfaction, except what is willed by God or connected with His will. Short of this essential detachment, no one can hope to enter into his inmost depths and experience the awakening of that inner self that is the dwelling of God, His hiding place, His temple, His stronghold, and His image.

The one who wants to know how to find God within himself receives the following answer from St. John of the Cross:

> Seek Him in faith and love, without desiring to find satisfaction in aught, or to taste and understand more than that which it is well for thee to know, for these two are the guides of the blind which will lead thee, by a way that thou knowest not, to the hidden place of God. Because faith, which is the secret that we have mentioned, is like the feet wherewith the soul journeys to God, and love is the guide that directs it. . . . Remain thou not therefore either partly or wholly in that which thy faculties can comprehend; I mean

be thou never willingly satisfied with that which thou understandest of God, but rather with that which thou understandest not of Him; and do thou never rest in loving and having delight in that which thou understandest or feelest concerning God, but do thou love and have delight in that which thou canst not understand or feel concerning Him; for this, as we have said, is to seek Him in faith. Since God is unapproachable and hidden, . . . however much it seem to thee that thou findest and feelest and understandest Him, thou must ever hold Him as hidden and serve him after a hidden manner, as one that is hidden. (*Spiritual Canticle* I, 11–12)

Yet at the end of this journey of faith and love which brings us into the depths of our own being and releases us that we may voyage beyond ourselves to God, the mystical life culminates in an experience of the presence of God that is beyond all description, and which is only possible because the soul has been completely "transformed in God" so as to become, so to speak, "one spirit" with Him. St. John of the Cross compares this revelation of God in the depths of our being to the "awakening" of the Word within us, a great stirring of supernatural and divine life, in which the Almighty One Who dwells in us is seen not as an inert "object," but is revealed in spirit and in power as the Ruler and Creator and Mover of all things. St. John says:

Even so, when a palace (the center of the soul) is thrown open a man may see at one and the same time the eminence of the person who is within the palace, and also what he is doing. And it is this, as I understand it, that happens in this awakening and glance of the soul. Though the soul is substantially in God, as is every creature, He draws back from before it some of the veils and curtains which are in front of it, so that it may see of what nature He is; and then there is revealed to it, and it is able to see (though somewhat darkly since not all the veils are drawn back) that face of His which is full of grace. And since it is moving all things by its power, there appears together with it that which it is doing, and it appears to move in them, and they in it, with continual movement; and for this reason the soul believes that God has moved and awakened, whereas that which has moved and awakened is in reality itself. (*Living Flame of Love,* IV, 7)

These are only a few characteristic texts in which Christian contemplatives have spoken of the awakening of the inner self and the consequent awareness of God. Since our inmost "I" is the perfect image of God, then when that "I" awakens, he finds within himself the Presence of Him Whose image he is. And, by a paradox beyond all human expression, God and the soul seem to have but one single "I." They are (by divine grace) as though one single person. They breathe and live and act as one. "Neither" of the "two" is seen as object.

To anyone who has full awareness of our "exile" from God, our alienation from this inmost self, and our blind wandering in the "region of unlikeness," this claim can hardly seem believable. Yet it is nothing else but the message of Christ calling us to awake from sleep, to return from exile, and find our true selves within ourselves, in that inner sanctuary which is His temple and His heaven, and (at the end of the prodigal's homecoming journey) the "Father's House."

THREE

Society and the Inner Self

So far, many of the texts we have quoted on the interior self give the false impression that this inner and spiritual identity is recovered merely by *isolation and*[1] introversion. This is far from correct. The inner self is not merely what remains when we turn away from exterior reality. It is not mere emptiness, or unconsciousness. On the contrary, if we imagine that our inmost self is purely and simply something in us that is *completely out of contact* with the world of exterior objects, we would condemn ourselves in advance to complete frustration in our quest for spiritual awareness. As a matter of fact, though a certain introversion and detachment are necessary in order to reestablish the proper conditions for the "awakening" of what is inmost in ourselves, the spiritual "I" obviously stands in a definite relationship to the world of objects. *All the more is it related to the world of other personal "subjects."*[2] In seeking to awaken the inner self we must try to learn how this relationship is entirely new and how it gives us a completely different view of things.

Instead of seeing the external world in its bewildering complexity, separateness, and multiplicity; instead of seeing objects as things to be manipulated for pleasure or profit; instead of placing ourselves over against objects in a posture of desire, defiance, suspicion, greed, or fear, the inner self sees the world from a deeper and more spiritual viewpoint. In the language of Zen, it sees things "without affirmation or denial," that is to say, from a higher vantage point which is intuitive and concrete and which has no need to manipulate or distort reality by means of slanted concepts and judgments. It simply "sees" what it sees and does not take refuge behind a screen of conceptual prejudices and verbalistic distortions. Example: the difference between a child's vision of a tree, which is utterly simple, uncolored by prejudice, and "new," and the lumberman's vision, entirely conditioned by profit motives and considerations of business. The lumberman is no doubt aware that the tree is beautiful, but this is a purely platonic and transient consideration compared with his habitual awareness that it can be reduced to a certain number of board feet at so much per foot. In this case, something is definitely "affirmed" which adds to and modifies one's vision of "a tree" or of a forest.

One of the Fathers of the oriental Church, Philoxenus of Mabbugh,[3] has an original and rather subtle view of original sin as a perversion of faith in which a false belief was superadded to the "simple" and unspoiled view of truth, so that direct knowledge became distorted by a false affirmation and negation. It is curious to realize that those who most deride religious faith are precisely the ones who interpose between themselves and reality a screen of beliefs based on an illusion of self-interest and of passionate attachment. The fact that these beliefs seem, pragmatically, to "work" is all the more fatal a deception. What, in fact, is the fruit of their working? Largely a perversion of the objects manipulated by the exterior man, and the even greater perversion of man himself. Such belief springs from, and increases, man's inner alienation.

In any case, the idea of Philoxenus presents a striking affinity with the epistemological bases of Zen Buddhism, which seeks above all to clear away the clouds of self-deception which we cast over external reality when we set ourselves to thinking about it. Zen seeks the direct, immediate view in which the experience of a subject-object duality is destroyed. That is why Zen resolutely refuses to answer clearly, abstractly, or dogmatically any religious or philosophical question whatever. Here is a typical example of one of those question-and-answer illustrations of Zen in which the masters deliberately frustrated all attempts of their disciples to slip an abstract doctrine in between the mind and the "this" which was right before their nose:

Someone asked Yakusan, who was sitting in meditation, "What are you doing here?"

He replied, "I am not doing anything."

"If so, you are sitting in idleness."

"Sitting in idleness is doing something."

"You say you are not doing anything, but what is this 'anything' that you are not doing?"

"Even the ancient sages know not," replied Yakusan. (Suzuki, *Studies in Zen*, p. 59)

And when disciples asked the Zen masters, "What is the meaning of Zen?" hoping for a doctrinal exposition, they would get in reply, "How do I know?" or "Ask the post over there." Or "Zen is that cypress tree in the courtyard!"

It is at once apparent that the exterior man tends to look at things from an economic or technical or hedonistic viewpoint which, in spite of all its pragmatic advantages, certainly removes the seer from direct contact with the reality which he sees. And this *exaggeration of* [4] the subject-object relationship by material interest or technical speculation is one of the main obstacles to contemplation, except of course in such notably exceptional cases as the intuitive and synthetic view which crowns and sums up the researches of an Einstein or of a Heisenberg. Einstein's view of the universe is one of the most notable "contemplative" achievements of our century, though in a special and limited sense of the word "contemplation." And here of course the vision was chiefly speculative rather than technological. And yet the atomic bomb owes its origin, in part, to such "contemplatives"!

Nor must we imagine that the inner vision is arrived at purely as the result of individual self-affirmation, in opposition to one's awareness of oneself as a member of a group or of mankind at large. Here again, the distinction is a matter of perspective. The discovery of our inner self is not arrived at merely by reflection on the fact that we "are not" any of "the others." This may be a part of it, no doubt, but it is not even the most essential part of the awareness. On the contrary, it is probably safe to say that no man could arrive at a genuine inner self-realization unless he had first become aware of himself as a member of a group—as an "I" confronted with a "Thou" who completes and fulfills his own being. In other words, the inner self sees the other not as a limitation upon itself, but as its complement, its "other self," and is even in a certain sense identified with that other, so that the two "are one." This unity in love is one of the most characteristic works of the inner self, so that paradoxically the inner "I" is not only isolated but at the same time united with others on a higher plane, which is in fact the plane of spiritual solitude. Here again, the level of "affirmation and negation" is transcended by spiritual awareness which is the work of love. And this is one of the most characteristic features of Christian contemplative awareness. The Christian is not merely "alone with the Alone" in the Neoplatonic sense, but he is One with all his "brothers in Christ." His inner self is, in fact, inseparable from Christ and hence it is in a mysterious and unique way inseparable from all the other "I's" who live in Christ, so that they all form one "Mystical Person," which is "Christ."

> That they all may be one as Thou Father in me and in Thee; that they also may be one in us; that the world may believe that Thou hast sent me. . . . I in them and Thou in me, that they may be made perfect in one . . . (John 17)

For this reason it is clear that Christian self-realization can never be a merely individualistic affirmation of one's isolated personality. The inner "I" is certainly the sanctuary of our most personal and individual solitude, and yet paradoxically it is precisely that which is most solitary and personal in ourselves which is united with the "Thou" who confronts us. We are not capable of union with one another on the deepest level until the inner self in each one of us is sufficiently awakened to confront the inmost spirit of the other. This mutual recognition is love "in the Spirit" and is effected, indeed, by the Holy Spirit. According to St. Paul, the inmost self of each one of us is our "spirit," or *pneuma,* or in other words the Spirit of Christ, indeed Christ Himself, dwelling in us. "For me to live is Christ." And by the spiritual recognition of Christ in our brother, we become "one in Christ" through the "bond of the Spirit." According to the mysterious phrase of St. Augustine, we then become "One Christ loving Himself."

In the same exegesis of Psalm 41 in which we have seen St. Augustine, above, speaking of the awakening of the inner self and the realization that God is to be found "above" that self, we also *discover*[5] this affirmation that God is to be found "through" and "above" the spiritual "self" of the faithful who are united in Him by charity. All these points must be carefully noted if we are not to be misled. First, Augustine nowhere says that God is to be found simply in the collectivity as such. Second, there is question of something more than a merely exterior and juridical society: rather, the mystical Christ is a spiritual body or organism whose life is charity. And by the power of this charity one is raised above and beyond the collective self of the faithful to God Who dwells in and above them all.

> How much is there I admire in this tabernacle (the Church):—the self-conquest and the virtues of God's servants. I admire the presence of those virtues in the soul. . . . (But he passes beyond the *tabernacle,* to the *House of God,* that is, from God dwelling in the saints to God in Himself.) And when I come to the House of God I am even struck dumb with astonishment. There, in the sanctuary of God, the House of God, is the fountain of understanding. It was in going up to the tabernacle that the Psalmist arrived at the House of God: by following the leadings of a certain delight, an inward mysterious and hidden pleasure, as if from the house of God there sounded sweetly some instrument; and he, whilst walking in the tabernacle, hearing a certain inward sound, led on by its sweetness and following the guidance of the sound, withdrawing himself from all noise of flesh and blood, made his way on even to the house of God. (Translation from Butler, *Western Mysticism,* p. 23)

Here it is quite clear that charity, which is the life and the awakening of the inner self, is in fact to a great extent awakened by the presence and the spiritual influence of other selves that are "in Christ." St. Augustine speaks of recognizing the inner self of other Christians through the virtuous actions which give evidence of the "Spirit" dwelling in them. It can be said that Christian "edification" is this mutual recognition of the inner spirit in one another, a recognition which is a manifestation of the Mystery of Christ.

In a word, the awakening of the inner self is purely the work of love, and there can be no love where there is not "another" to love. Furthermore, one does not awaken his inmost "I" merely by loving God alone, but by loving other men. Yet here again, as in the case of the inner awareness of contemplation described in the earlier passage, the necessary movement of transcendence must come and lift the spirit "above flesh and blood."

A love that is "above flesh and blood" is not something pale and without passion, but a love in which passion has been elevated and purified by selflessness, so that it no longer follows the inspiration of mere natural instinct. This love is guided by the Spirit of Christ and seeks the good of the other rather than our own momentary *interest or*[6] pleasure. More, even beyond all opposition between the profit of another and our own profit, it rests in love for love's own sake, and attains, in Christ, to the truth not insofar as it is desirable, but above all insofar as it is true and good in itself. This is at the same time our own highest good and the good of the others, and in such love as this, "all are One."

It would obviously be fatal to seek an inner awakening and self-realization purely and simply by withdrawal. Though a certain movement of withdrawal is necessary if we are to attain the perspective that solitude alone can open up to us, nevertheless this separation is in the interests of a higher union in which our solitude is not lost but perfected, because on this higher level there is no longer question of a love that can be manipulated or brought into subjection by flattery and base motives. Solitude is necessary for spiritual freedom. But once that freedom is acquired, it demands to be put to work in the service of a love in which there is no longer subjection or slavery. Mere withdrawal, without the return to freedom in the action, would lead to a static and deathlike inertia of the spirit in which the inner self would not awaken at all. There would be no light, no voice within us, only the silence and darkness of the tomb.

In contrast to the paradoxical recovery of unity in and beyond our own inner and solitary "I" is the false withdrawal of the exterior self within its own depths, a withdrawal which imprisons instead of liberating, and which makes impossible all real contact with the inner self of another. When I speak of the "exterior self" having "depths" of its own, I am perhaps pressing and complicating my metaphor beyond due limits. But I mean to make clear the fact that those recesses of the unconscious in which neurotic and psychotic derangement have their center belong in reality to man's exterior self: because the exterior self is not limited to consciousness. Freud's concept of the superego as an infantile and introjected substitute for conscience fits very well my idea of the exterior and alienated self. It is at once completely exterior and yet at the same time buried in unconsciousness. So too with the Freudian concept of the "id," insofar as it represents an automatic complex of drives toward pleasure or destruction in response to external stimuli.

I think this can go far to explain false mysticism and pseudo-religiosity. These are manifestations of a fake interiorization by which, instead of plunging into the depths of one's true freedom and spirituality, one simply withdraws into the darker subterranean levels of the exterior self, which remains alienated and subject to powers from the outside. The relation between this false inner self and external reality is entirely colored and perverted by a heavy and quasi-magical compulsivity. Instead of the freedom and spontaneity of an inner self that is entirely unpreoccupied with itself and goes forth to meet the other lightly and trustfully, without afterthought of self-concern, we have here the ponderous and obsessive delusion of the paranoid who lays claim to "magical" insight into others, and interprets the portentous "signs" he sees in external reality in favor of his own distended fears, lusts, and appetites for power. True Christian charity is stifled in such an atmosphere, and contemplation has no place in it. All is heavy, thick, biased, and dark with obsession, even though it lays claim to blinding and supernatural lights. It is a realm of dangerous appetites for command, of false visions and apocalyptic threats, of spiritual sensuality, and of a mysticism charged with undertones of sexual perversion.

Just as all sane men instinctively seek, in some way or other, the awakening of their true inner self, so all valid social forms of religion attempt, in some manner, to provide a situation in which each member of the worshiping group can rise above the group and above himself, to find himself and all the rest on a higher level. This implies that all truly serious and spiritual forms of religion aspire at least implicitly to a contemplative awakening both of the individual and of the group. But those forms of religious and liturgical worship which have lost their initial impulse of fervor tend more and more to forget their contemplative purpose, and to attach exclusive importance to rites and forms for their own sake, or for the sake of the effect which they are believed to exercise on the One Who is worshiped.

The highest form of religious worship finds its issue and fulfillment in contemplative awakening and in transcendent spiritual peace—in the quasi-experiential union of its members with God, beyond sense and beyond ecstasy. The lowest form is fulfilled in a numinous and magic sense of power which has been "produced" by rites and which gives one momentarily the chance to wring a magical effect from the placated deity. In between these two extremes are various levels of ecstasy, exaltation, ethical self-fulfillment, juridical righteousness, and aesthetic intuition. In all these various ways, religion primitive and sophisticated, crude and pure, active and contemplative, seeks to attain to the inner awakening, or at least to produce an apparently satisfactory substitute for it.

But it is evident from what has been said above that few religions ever really penetrate to the inmost soul of the believer, and even the highest of them do not, in their social and liturgical forms, invariably reach the inmost "I" of each participant. The common level of inferior religion is situated somewhere in the collective subconscious of the worshipers, and perhaps more often than not in a *collective exterior self.* This is certainly a verifiable fact in modern totalitarian pseudo-religions of state and class. And this is one of the most dangerous features of our modern barbarism: the invasion of the world by a barbarity from within society and within man himself. Or rather, the reduction of man, in technological society, to a level of almost pure alienation in which he can be brought at will, any time, to a kind of political ecstasy, carried away by the hate, the fear, and the crude aspirations centered about a leader, a propaganda slogan, or a political symbol. That this sort of ecstasy is to some extent "satisfactory" and produces a kind of pseudo-spiritual catharsis, or at least a release of tension, is unfortunately all too often verified. And it is what modern man is coming more and more to accept as an ersatz for genuine religious fulfillment, for moral activity, and for contemplation itself.

It is becoming more and more common for the innate aspiration which all men, as images of God, share for the recovery of their inmost self to be perverted and satisfied by the mere parody of religious mystery and the evocation of a collective shadow of a "self." The mere fact that the discovery of this ersatz interiority is *unconscious*[7] seems to be sufficient to make it acceptable. It "feels like" spontaneity, and above all there is the meretricious assurance of greatness and infallibility, and the sweet loss of personal responsibility which one enjoys by abandoning himself to a collective mood, no matter how murderous or how vile it may be in itself. This would seem to be in all technical reality what the New Testament speaks of as Antichrist—that pseudo-Christ in which all real selves are lost and everything is enslaved to a pale, ferocious *imago* inhabiting the maddened group.

It is important at all times to keep clear the distinction between true and false religion, true and false interiority, holiness and possession, love and frenzy, contemplation and magic. In every case, there is an aspiration toward inner awakening, and the same means, good or indifferent in themselves, may be used for good or evil, health or sickness, freedom or obsession.

Symbolism plays a constant and universal part in all religious activity oriented toward some inner awakening. The awakening itself is signified, or myths which express it are represented, in art, rites, sacred gesture, dance, music. Hieratic songs and prayers surround the central act of sacrifice, itself usually deeply symbolic. Higher forms of religion embody the awakening and the union of the spirit with God in a "mystery" where the ritual enactment of a myth serves as "initiation" to a spiritual life *or a consummation*[8] in union with the god.

But only in the highest and most spiritual worship does the real connection between exterior rite and inner awakening remain definite and clear. As religion loses its fervor and becomes stereotyped, the worshiper lives and moves on a level where faith is too weak and too diffuse to lead to any inner awakening. Instead of appealing to the inmost self, religion that has thus grown tired is content to stir up the unconscious emotions of the exterior self. In this case there is no real inner awakening, and the reassurance conceived in ritual worship is no longer spiritual, personal, and free.

The Old Testament prophets inveighed against this more or less exterior worship, which activated the lips but not the heart, and Christ Himself rebuked it in the Pharisees. All genuine revivals of religious fervor aim, in one way or another, at restoring the deeply interior orientation of religious activity, and attempt a renewal and purification of the interior life generated by symbolic rites, mysteries, and prayers. It is a question of getting rid of mechanical and compulsive formalism and awakening the inner, spontaneous fervor of "the heart." Generally speaking, the "heart" is used as a more or less adequate symbol of the inner self, though in the Old Testament other physical organs are substituted for it indifferently, for instance, the viscera and the "reins."[9] Unfortunately this haphazard use of a physical symbol to localize the source of religious spontaneity is no guarantee against emotional, sentimental, erotic, and even bacchanalian substitutes for the awakening of the inner self.

As worship degenerates, there is an ever increasing tendency to make use of stimulating agencies to break down the inhibitions generated by routine and restore a semblance of life and power to the symbolic rites. Hence the use of alcohol and of drugs to obtain a spiritual release. But the "inner self" thus released is not necessarily the "I," but rather more usually the subconscious libido held in check automatically by conscience, habit, convention, taboo, or magical fear. The release thus achieved is material rather than spiritual, and its effect is an explosion of *psychic*[10] energy which may be salutary or noxious, *painful or happy,*[11] according to circumstance.

Here too we may remark on the gradual, progressive degeneration and brutalization of symbols that lose their religious "kick." Study of the religions of Mexico suggests a development that began with a highly spiritualized and refined worship, with cosmic contemplative possibilities and sacrifices of *fruits of the earth,*[12] and developed bit by bit into the bloodthirsty warrior cult of the Aztecs, centered on war and on human sacrifice. The Aztec sacrifice of the human heart to the sun suggests a kind of frightful parody of the pure and spiritual manifestation of the "inmost self." Here, instead of a man offering to God the "sacrifice" of his exterior self, by self-forgetfulness and love, in order to release and manifest before the face of God the hidden face of his interior soul, a victim is seized by the hieratic representative of collective ferocity, and his heart, cut out with an obsidian knife, is held up bleeding to satisfy the hunger of the sun! This

example offers us much food for meditation today, as we fall back into collective barbarism in which the individual and his freedom once again lose
their meaning and each man is only an expendable unit ready to be
immolated to the *political idols*[13] on which the prosperity and power of the
collectivity *seem to*[14] depend.

Nevertheless, it is clear that such examples must not be used to justify
rash generalizations about primitive and "pagan" religion. Everywhere, in
all kinds of religion, we find the high and the low, the spiritual and gross,
the beautiful and the obscene. If, on the one hand, there are Bacchic orgies
of drunken women and if temple prostitution substitutes, in certain fertil-
ity cults, for the discovery of our own intimate contemplative secret, on
the other hand, there are pure and sublime mysteries and, especially in the
Far East, utterly sophisticated and refined forms of spiritual contemplation.
The religion of Abraham indeed was primitive, and it hovered, for a terrible moment, over the abyss of human sacrifice. Yet Abraham walked with
God in simplicity and peace, and the example of his faith (precisely in the
case of Isaac) furnished material for the meditations of the most sophisticated religious thinker of the last century, the father of existentialism,
Søren Kierkegaard.[15]

Among the Sioux Indians, together with a very rich and varied liturgical life, we find the curiously moving individual and contemplative mystery of "crying for a vision." In this, a young man, following no communal
prejudice but only personal and spontaneous inspiration, is prepared by
prayers and ceremonies and then goes off to spend several days in prayer
and solitude on a mountain, seeking an "answer" from the Great Spirit. It
is recorded that deep and genuine examples of inner awakening and even
of (natural) quasi-prophetic vocations have been granted to Indians in this
primitive spiritual exercise.

It is well known that in the Orient, in China, India, Japan, and Indo-
nesia, the religious and contemplative life has been fostered for centuries
and has known a development of unparalleled richness. Asia has for centuries been a continent of great monastic communities. At the same time
the solitary life has flourished, either in the shadow of the monasteries or
in the wilderness of jungle, mountain, or desert. Hindu yoga, in its various

forms, has become almost legendary of Eastern contemplation. Yoga makes use of a variety of disciplines and ascetic techniques for the "liberation" of man's spirit from the limitations imposed upon him by material, bodily existence. Everywhere in the East, whether in Hinduism or Buddhism, we find that deep, unutterable thirst for the rivers of Paradise. Whatever may be the philosophies and theologies behind these forms of contemplative existence, the striving is always the same: the quest for unity, a return to the inmost self united with the Absolute, a quest for Him Who is above all, and in all, and Who Alone is Alone. Nor is it correct to accuse the oriental mystic of selfishness, as is too frequently done. He too seeks, in his own way, the redemption of all living beings. He too, like St. Paul, is well aware of the fact that:

The expectation of the creature waiteth for the revelation of the sons of God, for the creature was made subject to vanity. . . . But the creature also itself shall be delivered from the servitude of corruption, into the liberty of the glory of the children of God. (Romans 8:19–21)

Note the analogies between Paul's term "servitude of corruption" and the Hindu concept of karma.[16] There are other facile generalizations about Hindu religion current in the West which it would be well to take with extreme reserve: for instance, the statement that for the Hindu there is no "personal God." On the contrary, the mysticism of bhakti yoga is a mysticism of affective devotion and of ecstatic union with God under the most personal and human forms, sometimes very reminiscent of the "bridal mysticism" of so many Western mystics. And it must be said that it is generally neither fair nor enlightening to criticize this or any other form of yoga purely on the basis of a Western and especially an Aristotelian metaphysic, since there is perhaps very little common ground between them. This does not mean that the differences between Hinduism and Christianity are of no significance and can be waved aside without further concern, but only that they are difficult to understand and to explain correctly and that the ground for such an explanation has perhaps not yet been fully prepared.

It is certain that the Bhagavad Gita[17] is just as much entitled to a place in a college course on humanities as Plato or Homer, and it is a wonder that the lofty religious literature of the East has not been numbered among the

"Great Books" which now form the basis of a liberal education at least in America. [*This omission is no longer pardonable.*][18] The *Gita,* an ancient Sanskrit philosophical poem, preaches a contemplative way of serenity, detachment, and personal devotion to God, under the form of the Lord Krishna, and expressed most of all in detached activity—work done without concern for results but with the pure intention of fulfilling the will of God. It is a doctrine of pure love resembling in many points that preached by St. Bernard, Tauler, Fenelon, and many other Western mystics. It implies detachment even from the joys of contemplation, as from all earthly and temporal achievements. What we have to say later about "masked contemplation"[19] may perhaps be something like the doctrine of contemplation-hidden-in-action, which seems to be the very heart of the *Bhagavad Gita.* The contemplative recognition of the inmost self, or rather peace in the "unknowing" which emanates from the inmost self, is what the *Gita* knows as yoga. See:

> *Steadfast a lamp burns sheltered from the wind;*
> *Such is the likeness of the Yogi's mind*
> *Shut from sense storms and burning bright to heaven.*
> *When the mind broods placid, soothed with holy wont,*
> *When Self contemplates self, and in itself*
> *Hath comfort; when it knows the nameless joy*
> *Beyond all scope of sense, revealed to soul—*
> *Only to soul, and knowing wavers not*
> *True to the farther Truth . . .*
> *. . . Call that state "peace"*
> *That happy severance "yoga."*
> *(Bk. VI, translation of Sir Edward Arnold)*

We are in a position, I think, to interpret this text correctly when we reflect that the yogi is not an exterior self mirrored in his own ego, but one who has found that inner self in whom God Himself dwells and is manifest. The verses can easily be harmonized with St. Augustine, due allowance being made for divergences in ontological theory.

This passage of the *Gita* is one which reminds us of Patanjali, the greatest yogi, whose *raja yoga* is the Indian opposite number of the apophatic mysticism of the West, represented by St. Gregory of Nyssa, Pseudo-Dionysius, and St. John of the Cross. The object of *raja yoga* is to attain, by control of the thoughts, first to a state of higher spiritual consciousness (*purusha*) and beyond that to *samadhi* (meditation without further "seed" of conceptual thought). Later in this book when we speak of "active contemplation," we refer to something akin to *purusha,* and to what the Greek Fathers called *theoria physica.* And when we speak of "infused contemplation," we refer to a more supernatural form of *samadhi* which the Greek Fathers called *theologia,* mystical theology or pure contemplatión beyond all thought.

In Asia, contemplation has not generally been regarded as an aristocratic privilege. On the contrary, it used to be common for ordinary married people in India to separate, in advancing age, and live in solitary contemplation to prepare for the end of this life. And it is well known that Asia has long been the most thriving home of monastic vocations. Indeed, in Asia it can be said, perhaps not without cause in many cases, that monasticism has become so familiar as to breed contempt.

It may be remarked in parentheses that theologians generally regard the spiritual experiences of oriental religion as occurring on the natural rather than on the supernatural level. However, they have often admitted, with Jacques Maritain and Fr. Garrigou-Lagrange,[20] that truly supernatural and mystical contemplation is certainly possible outside the visible church, since God is the master of His gifts and wherever there is sincerity and an earnest desire for truth, He will not deny the gifts of His grace. As we grow in knowledge and appreciation of oriental religion we will come to realize the depth and richness of its varied forms of contemplation. Up to the present, our judgments have been too vague and too undocumented and have borne witness chiefly to our own ignorance. However, this statement is not intended as an encouragement to the foolish and equally ignorant infatuation with oriental cults which tends to be fashionable in certain circles today.

In classical Greece, contemplation was definitely aristocratic and intellectual. It was the privilege of a philosophical minority, for whom it was a matter of study and reflection rather than of prayer. But the classical Greek idea of contemplation, for all its beauty, is one-sided and incomplete. The contemplative (*theoretikos*) is a man of leisure who devotes himself to study and reasoned reflection in the quest of pure truth. The contemplative life is a life of intellectual speculation, and perhaps of debate. It is the life of the academy, the university. The contemplative is the professional philosopher. But in such a concept, the essentially religious aspect of contemplation tends to get lost. Furthermore, here the "erotic" desire for contemplation of truth as a "highest good" that can give man "perfect happiness" tends to become too hedonistic and therefore to defeat its own ends. We have seen in the first pages of this essay that a hedonistic quest for contemplation is doomed to frustration.

The Christian contemplative tradition owes much, however, to classical Greece. The Christian Platonists of Alexandria (especially Origen and Clement) adopted something of the intellectual hedonism of Plato, and as a result we still tend to think of the contemplative life, unconsciously, as one of ease, aestheticism, and speculation.

The great practitioners of contemplation who were the Desert Fathers of Egypt[21] and the Near East did their best to dispel the illusion. They went into the desert not to seek pure spiritual beauty or an intellectual light, but to see the Face of God. And they knew that before they could see His Face, they would have to struggle, instead, with His adversary. They would have to cast out the devil subtly lodged in their exterior self. They went into the desert not to study speculative truth, but to wrestle with practical evil; not to perfect their analytical intelligence, but to purify their hearts. They went into solitude not to *get* something, but in order to *give themselves,* for "He that would save his life must lose it, and he that will lose his life, for the sake of Christ, shall save it." By their renunciation of passion and attachment, their crucifixion of the exterior self, they liberated the inner man, the new man "in Christ."

The fact that "contemplation" (*theoria*) is not mentioned in the New Testament should not mislead us. We shall see presently that the teaching of Christ is essentially "contemplative" in a much higher, more practical, and less esoteric sense than Plato's.

In the Christian tradition, as we have already observed, contemplation is simply the "experience" (or, better, the quasi-experiential knowledge) of

God in a luminous darkness which is the perfection of faith illuminating our inmost self. It is the "meeting" of the spirit with God in a communion of love and understanding which is a gift of the Holy Spirit and a penetration into the Mystery of Christ. The word "contemplation" suggests lingering enjoyment, timelessness, and a kind of suave passivity. All these elements are there, but they smack rather of pagan *theoria*. The important thing in contemplation is not enjoyment, not pleasure, not happiness, not peace, but the transcendent experience of reality and truth in the act of a supreme and liberated spiritual love. The important thing in contemplation is not gratification and rest, but awareness, life, creativity, and freedom. In fact, contemplation is man's highest and most essential spiritual activity. It is his most creative and dynamic affirmation of his divine sonship. It is not just the sleepy, suave, restful embrace of "being" in a dark, generalized contentment: it is a flash of the lightning of divinity piercing the darkness of nothingness and sin. Not something general and abstract, but something, on the contrary, as concrete, particular, and "existential" as it can possibly be. It is the confrontation of man with his God, of the Son with His Father. It is the awakening of Christ within us, the establishment of the Kingdom of God in our own soul, the triumph of the Truth and of Divine Freedom in the inmost "I" in which the Father becomes one with the Son in the Spirit Who is given to the believer.

[FOUR]

Christian Contemplation

The story of Adam's fall from Paradise says, in symbolic terms, that man was created as a contemplative. The fall from Paradise was a fall from unity. The Platonizing Greek Fathers even taught that the division of humanity into two sexes was a result of the Fall. St. Augustine, in a more cautious and psychological application of the narrative, says that in the Fall Adam, man's interior and spiritual self, his contemplative self, was led astray by Eve, his exterior, material, and practical self, his active self. Man fell from the unity of contemplative vision into the multiplicity, complication, and distraction of an active, worldly existence.

Since he was now dependent entirely on exterior and contingent things, he became an exile in a world of objects, each one capable of deluding and enslaving him. Centered no longer in God and in his inmost, spiritual self, man now had to *see* and *be aware* of himself as if he were his own god. He had to study himself as a kind of pseudo-object, from which he was estranged. And to compensate for the labors and frustrations of this estrangement, he must try to admire, assert, and gratify himself at the expense of others like himself. Hence the complex and painful network of loves and hatreds, desires and fears, lies and excuses in which we are all held captive. In such a condition, man's mind is enslaved by an inexorable concern with all that is exterior, transient, illusory, and trivial. And carried away by his pursuit of alien shadows and forms, he can no longer see his own true inner "face," or recognize his identity in the spirit and in God, for that identity is secret, invisible, and incommunicable. But man has lost the courage and the faith without which he cannot be content to be "unseen." He is pitifully dependent on self-observation and self-assertion. That is to say, he is utterly exiled from God and from his own true self, for neither in God nor in our inmost self can there be any aggressive self-assertion: there is only the plain presence of love and of truth.

So man is exiled from God and from his inmost self. He is tempted to seek God, and happiness, outside himself. So his quest for happiness becomes, in fact, a flight from God and from himself: a flight that takes him further and further away from reality. In the end, he has to dwell in the "region of unlikeness"—having lost his inner resemblance to God in losing his freedom to enter his own home, which is the sanctuary of God.

But man must return to Paradise. He must recover himself, salvage his dignity, recollect his lost wits, return to his true identity. There is only one way in which this could be done, says the Gospel of Christ. God Himself must come, like the woman in the parable seeking the lost groat. God Himself must become Man, in order that, in the Man-God, man might be able to lose himself as man and find himself as God. God Himself must die on the Cross, leaving man a pattern and a proof of His infinite love. And man, communing with God in the death and resurrection of Christ, must die the spiritual death in which his exterior self is destroyed and his inner self rises from death by faith and lives again "unto God." He must taste eternal life, which is "to know the Father, the one true God, and Jesus Christ whom He has sent."[1]

The Christian life is a return to the Father, the Source, the Ground of all existence, through the Son, the Splendor and the Image of the Father, in the Holy Spirit, the Love of the Father and the Son. And this return is only possible by detachment and "death" in the exterior self, so that the inner self, purified and renewed, can fulfill its function as image of the Divine Trinity.

Christianity is life and wisdom in Christ. It is a return to the Father in Christ. It is a return to the infinite abyss of pure reality in which our own reality is grounded, and in which we exist. It is a return to the source of all meaning and all truth. It is a return to the inmost springs of life and joy. It is a rediscovery of paradise within our own spirit by self-forgetfulness. And, because of our oneness with Christ, it is the recognition of ourselves as sons of the Father. It is the recognition of ourselves as other Christs. It is the awareness of strength and love imparted to us by the miraculous presence of the Nameless and Hidden One Whom we call the Holy Spirit.

(The Father is a Holy Spirit, but He is named Father. The Son is a Holy Spirit, but He is named Son. The Holy Spirit has a name which is known only to the Father and the Son. But can it be that when He takes us to Himself and unites us to the Father through the Son, He takes upon Himself, in us, our own secret name? Is it possible that his ineffable Name becomes our own? Is it possible that we can come to know, for ourselves, the Name of the Holy Spirit when we receive from Him the revelation of our own identity in Him? I can ask these questions, but not answer them.)

1. Contemplation and Theology

Most non-Christians, and probably also many Protestant Christians, probably suppose that the intense preoccupation of the early Church Fathers with the technical details of the dogma of the Incarnation was a matter of arbitrary and subjective willfulness, and that it had little objective importance. But, as a matter of fact, the intricacies of Christology and of the dogma of the hypostatic union were by no means a mere authoritarian web devised to capture the minds and to keep in subjection the wills of the faithful, as rationalism glibly used to declare. Both the theologian and the ordinary believer, in the Patristic age, realized the importance of the correct theological formulation of the mystery of the Incarnation, because dogmatic error would in fact imply disastrous practical consequences in the spiritual life of each individual Christian.

One of the main reasons why St. Athanasius[2] so stubbornly defended the divinity of Christ against the Arians, who at one time outnumbered the orthodox Christians by a vast majority, was that he saw that if Christ were not God, then it followed that the Christian hope for union with God in and through Christ was a delusion. Everything, as St. Paul himself had declared equivalently, depended on faith in Christ as the true Son of God, the Word Incarnate. "For if Christ be not risen again then our preaching is vain, and your faith also is vain. Yea and also we are found false witnesses of God, because we have given testimony against God" (1 Corinthians 15:14–15).

It may perhaps not be clear at first sight what this belief in the Resurrection might have to do with contemplation. But in fact the Resurrection and Ascension of Christ, the New Adam, completely restored human nature to its spiritual condition and made possible the divinization of every man coming into the world. This meant that in each one of us the inner self was now able to be awakened and transformed by the action of the Holy Spirit, and this awakening would not only enable us to discover our true identity "in Christ," but would also make the living and Risen Savior present in us. Hence the importance of the Divinity of Christ—for it is as God-Man that He is risen from the dead and as God-Man that He is capable of living and acting in us all by His Spirit, so that in Him we are not only our true personal selves, but are also one Mystical Person, one Christ. And thus each one of us is endowed with the creative liberty of the Son of God. Each one of us, in some sense, is able to be completely transformed into the likeness of Christ, to become, as He is, divinely human, and thus to share His spiritual authority and charismatic power in the world.

It is significant that, among the minority of Christians who stood with Athanasius, the contemplative Desert Fathers formed a solid and unyielding phalanx of believers in the divinity of the Second Person and the Incarnation of the Word. For they believed, with all the orthodox Fathers, what St. Athanasius succinctly declared in the formula, *borrowed from St. Irenaeus:*[3] "God became man in order that man might become God."

If the Word emerged from the depths of the unknowable mystery of the Father, "Whom no man hath seen at any time," it was not merely in order to have mankind cast itself down at His feet. He came to be a man like ourselves and, in His own Person, to unite man to God. As a result of this union of God and Man in the one Person of Christ it was possible for every man to be united to God in his own person, as a true son of God, not by nature but by adoption.

If the "Son of Man came to seek and to save that which was lost," this was not merely in order to reestablish man in a favorable juridical position with regard to God: it was to elevate, change, and transform man into God, in order that God might be revealed in Man, and that all men might become One Son of God in Christ. The New Testament texts in which this mystery is stated are unequivocal, and yet they have been to a very great extent ignored not only by the faithful, but also by theologians.

The Greek and Latin Fathers never made this mistake! For them, the mystery of the hypostatic union, or the union of the divine and human natures in the One Person of the Word, the God-Man, Jesus Christ, was not only a truth of the greatest, most revolutionary, and most existential actuality, but it was the central truth of all being and all history. It was the key which alone could unlock the meaning of everything else and reveal the inner and spiritual significance of man, of his actions as an individual and in society, of history, of the world, and of the whole cosmos.

If in Christ the assumed human nature, which is in every respect literally and perfectly human, belongs to the Person of the Word of God, then everything human in Christ is by that very fact divine. His thoughts, actions, and His very existence are the works and existence of a divine Person. In Him, we see a Man in every respect identical with ourselves as far as His nature is concerned, thinking and feeling and acting according to our nature, and yet at the very same time living on a completely transcendent and divine level of consciousness and of being. For His consciousness and His being are the consciousness and being of God Himself. Of course, the Living Christ, now enthroned at the right hand of the Father in eternity (according to the metaphorical language of the Scriptures), is indeed in a state of being which to us is beyond all capacity to express or to imagine, and yet in this state of being He is also truly and literally human as well as divine, and there is *no cleavage* between His divine and human natures. Nor was there even the slightest split between the humanity and the divinity of Christ in that other historical state of being in which He lived on this earth. Though the two natures were not confused in any way, they were still completely *one*[4] in Him, as completely as our own body and soul are one in us.

The very first step to a correct understanding of the Christian theology of contemplation is to grasp clearly the unity of God and man in Christ, which of course presupposes the equally crucial unity of man in himself.

For the soul and body are not divided against one another as good and evil principles; and our salvation by no means consists of a rejection of the body in order to liberate the soul from the dominance of an evil material principle. On the contrary, our body is as much ourselves as the soul, and neither one without the other can claim to exist purely in its own right, as a true personal being. It was the same also in Christ, in Whom the life, being, and actions of His Body were just as much His own, and just as much divine, as the thoughts and aspiration of His soul. So when Christ walked down the roads of Galilee, it was not an illusory man or even a real man acting as a temporary "front" for a Divine Agent: the Man Himself Who walked there was God.

In the words of St. Maximus the Confessor:[5]

> The superessential Word, clothing Himself at the time of His ineffable conception with all that is in our nature, possessed nothing human that was not at the same time divine. . . . The knowledge of these things is indemonstrable, being beyond understanding and perceptible only to the faith of those who honor the mystery of Christ in the sincerity of their heart. (*Ambigua, Patrologia Graeca*, 91.1053)

And again:

> The mystery of the Incarnation of the Word contains in itself all the meaning of the enigmas and symbols of Scripture, all the significance of visible and intelligible creatures. He who knows the mystery of the Cross and the Sepulchre knows the reason (logos) of all things. He who is initiated into the hidden meaning of the resurrection, knows the end for which, from the beginning, God created all things. (*Centuriae Gnosticae, Patrologia Graeca*, 90.1108)

The fact that since the Incarnation God and Man have become inseparable in the One Person of Jesus Christ means that the "supernatural order" has not just been somehow imposed from without upon created nature, but that nature itself has, in man, become transformed and supernaturalized so that in everyone in whom Christ lives and acts, by the Holy Spirit, there is no longer any further division between nature and supernature. The man who lives and acts according to the grace of Christ dwelling in him acts in that case as another Christ, as a son of God, and thus he prolongs in his own life the effects and the miracle of the Incarnation. In the words of St. Maximus: "God desires at all times to make Himself man in those who are worthy" (*Quaestiones ad Thalassium, Patrologia Graeca* 90.321).

But this, for the Greek Fathers, clearly means a higher and nobler level of life than we ordinarily lead. It means a life purified, liberated by the action of the Holy Spirit, a life enlightened by supernatural contemplation. Of course, Christ has taken possession of our souls and bodies, and we are already divinized, in the roots of our being, by Baptism. But this divine life remains hidden and dormant within us unless it is more fully developed by a life of asceticism and charity and, on a higher level, of contemplation. We not only passively receive in us the grace of Christ, but we actively renew in our own life the self-emptying and self-transformation by which God became man. Just as the Word "emptied Himself" of His divine and transcendent nobility in order to "descend" to the level of man, so we must empty ourselves of what is human in the ignoble sense of the word, which really means less than human, in order that we may become God. This does not mean the sacrifice or destruction of anything that really belongs to our human nature as it was assumed by Christ, but it means the complete, radical cutting off of everything in us that was *not* assumed by Him because it was not capable of being divinized. And what is this? It is everything that is *focused*[6] on our exterior and self-centered passion as self-assertion, greed, lust; as the desire for the survival and perpetuation of our illusory and superficial self, to the detriment of our interior and true self. But our inner man is "renewed in Christ" to become the "new man." As St. Paul says:

> Though our outward man is corrupted, our inward man is renewed from day to day . . . while we look not at the things which are seen, but at the things which are not seen. (2 Corinthians 4:16, 18)

> Strip yourselves of the old man, with his deeds and put on the new, him who is *renewed unto knowledge* according to the image of Him that created him. (Colossians 3:9, 10)

That God would grant you . . . to be strengthened by His Spirit with might unto the inward man, that Christ may dwell by faith in your hearts: that being rooted and founded in charity you may be able to comprehend with all the saints what is the breadth and length and height and depth, to know also the charity of Christ which surpasseth all knowledge that you may be filled unto all the fullness of God. (Ephesians 3:16–19)

These texts already give us a full and profound picture of the idea of contemplation that fills the New Testament everywhere, though the term is never mentioned in this particular sense. It is a question of the inward man springing to life at the spiritual contact of God, in faith. This contact brings one face-to-face with a reality that is "unseen," first of all, and yet, paradoxically, this "seeing" of the "unseen" brings about an ever deepening renewal of life which is "according to knowledge," that is to say, according to a genuine experience of Christ, caused by our likeness, or "sonship," by the gift of the divine Spirit Who makes Christ "dwell in our hearts" or in our inmost selves. The result of this indwelling of Christ and of the Holy Spirit is the overflowing fullness of new life, of charity, divine love, and a spiritual comprehension of the mystery of God's life within us in all its dimensions, through the experience of Christ's love for us "which sur-passes all understanding."

Later in the book we shall return to these fundamental ideas about Christian contemplation as an experiential contact with God, in and through Christ, beyond all knowledge, in the darkness of the mystery of divine charity, in "unknowing." At the moment it is sufficient to say cate-gorically that this contemplation is a deep participation in the Christ-life, a spiritual sharing in the union of God and Man which is the hypostatic union. This is the whole meaning of the doctrine of divine sonship, of our being sons of God in Christ and having the Spirit of Christ.

For whoever are led by the Spirit of God, they are the sons of God. For you have not received the spirit of bondage again in fear, but you have received the spirit of adoption of sons whereby we cry Abba, Father. For the Spirit Himself giveth testimony to our spirit that we are the sons of God. (Romans 8:14–16)

This "testimony of the Spirit" to our inmost self (our own spirit) is in a very broad sense what we call "contemplation" in the Christian context.

2. Contemplation and the Gospels

Let us now briefly and succinctly examine some of the most important Gospel texts related to our subject. First of all, Jesus declared unequivocally that He and the Father were one, and that he was the Son of God in the strictest and most literal sense of the word. For this He was put to death.

> I and the Father are One. . . . I am the Son of God. . . . If I do not the works of my Father believe me not. But if I do, though you will not believe me, believe the works: that you may know and believe that the Father is in me and I am in the Father. (John 10:30, 36–38)

> I am the light of the world: he that followeth me walketh not in darkness but shall have the light of life. . . . I am not alone, but I and the Father that sent me. . . . You are of this world, I am not of this world. . . . I am the beginning who also speak unto you. . . . He that sent me is true, and the things I hear from Him, these same I speak in the world. . . . I do nothing of myself, but as the Father hath taught me, these things I speak. And He that sent me is with me, and he hath not left me alone: for I do always the things that please Him. . . . From God I proceeded and came: for I came not of myself, but He sent me. . . . If any man keep my word he shall not see death forever. . . . If I glorify myself my glory is nothing. It is my Father that glorifieth me, of whom you say that He is your God. And you have not known Him, but I know Him. . . . I do know Him, and do keep His word. Abraham your Father rejoiced that he might see my day: he saw it and was glad. . . . Amen, amen I say to you, before Abraham was made, I am. (John 8)

> Have I been so long a time with you and have you not known me? . . . He that seeth me seeth the Father also. . . . I am the way, the truth and the life. No man cometh to the Father but by me. . . . Do you not believe that I am in the Father and the Father in me? The words that I speak to you, I speak not of myself. But the Father who abideth in me, He doth the works. (John 14)

These texts are clear enough. And there is no question about the way they have been interpreted by twenty centuries of Christian tradition. Christian contemplation is based on faith in this mystery. If Christ came into the world as the Son of God, and if the Father was present in Him: if Christ has left the world and gone to the Father, how do we "see" Him, or bridge the gap that remains between us and the transcendental remoteness of His mystery in heaven? The answer is that the Word, in the Father, is not only transcendentally removed at an infinite distance above us, but also and at the same time He is immanent in our world, first of all by nature as the Creator of the world, but then in a special dynamic and mystical presence as the Savior, Redeemer, and Lover of the world. The point is, then, to know how we enter into contact with this special presence of the Lord in His cosmos and in our hearts. If in St. John's terms we have to become the sons of God, and in order to become the sons of God we have to receive Christ, then how do we receive Christ?

The answer is, *by faith:* and this means not simply by an intellectual assent to certain authoritative dogmatic propositions, but, more than that, by *the commitment of our whole self and of our whole life to the reality of the presence of Christ in the world.* This act of total surrender is not simply a fantastic intellectual and mystical gamble; it is something much more serious: it is an act of love for this unseen Person Who, in the very gift of love by which we surrender ourselves to His reality, also makes Himself present to us. The union of our mind, spirit, and life with the Word present within us is effected by the Holy Spirit.

All this is clear in Christ's discourse at the Last Supper, His spiritual testament.[7] First, a distinction is made between the physical presence of the Lord with which the disciples had become familiar during the period when He lived among them on earth and the new more intimate invisible presence which would be His when He had died on the Cross, risen from the dead, and established His Kingdom.

> But I tell you the truth, it is expedient for you that I go: for if I go not the Paraclete will not come to you: but if I go I will send Him to you. . . . When He, the Spirit of Truth, is come, He will teach you all truth. . . . He shall glorify me because he shall receive of mine and shall show it to you. (John 16:7, 13, 14)

These words need to be completed by an explanation from the First Epistle of St. John: at the same time, we just remember what was said above by St. Paul about the Holy Spirit making Christ present to the Christian soul. St. John says:

You have the unction from the Holy One and know all things. . . . Let the unction which you have received from Him abide in you. And you have no need that any man teach you; but as His unction teaches you of all things, and is truth and no lie. And as it hath taught you, abide in Him. (1 John 2:20, 27)

It is evident, then, that the Holy Spirit is given to us as a true and literal gift of God: *Donum Dei altissimi*.[8] He is truly, as St. Thomas says, our possession, which means to say He becomes, as it were, our own spirit, speaking within our own being. It is He that becomes, as it were, our spiritual and divine self, and by virtue of His presence and inspirations we are and we act as other Christs. By Him and through Him we are transformed in Christ. It is clear from the Gospels and Epistles of the New Testament that the Holy Spirit is truly meant to be given to us as a personal principle of love and activity in the supernatural order, transforming us in Christ. The life of contemplation is, then, not simply a life of human technique and discipline; it is the life of the Holy Spirit in our inmost souls. The whole duty of the contemplative is to abandon what is base and trivial in his own life, and do all he can to conform himself to the secret and obscure promptings of the Spirit of God. This of course requires a constant discipline of humility, obedience, self-distrust, prudence, and above all faith.

St. Paul earnestly wanted all his Corinthian converts to receive the Holy Spirit and be guided by Him. He tells them in no uncertain words:

We speak the wisdom of God in mystery, a wisdom which is hidden, which God ordained before the world, unto our glory. . . . To us God hath revealed (hidden things) by His Spirit, for the Spirit searcheth all things, even the deep things of God. For what man knoweth the things of a man but the spirit of a man that is in him? So the things also that are of God no man knoweth, but the Spirit of God. Now we have received the spirit not of this world, but the Spirit that is of God; that we may know the things that are given us from God. (1 Corinthians 2:7, 10–12)

This is an important witness to the New Testament idea of what we call contemplation of God. Just as a man knows himself by the testimony of his own inmost self, his own spirit, so God reveals Himself in the love of His Spirit. And this Spirit of God, dwelling in us, given to us, to be as it were our own Spirit, enables us to know and experience, in a mysterious manner, the reality and presence of the divine mercy in ourselves. So the Holy Spirit is intimately united to our own inmost self, and His presence in us makes our "I" the "I" of Christ and of God.

This is the Holy Spirit Whom Christ Himself promised to His disciples and to us at the Last Supper. Too often these texts are merely taken in a broad impersonal sense: the Holy Spirit was given to the Apostles, and hence to the Church. This means that the Holy Spirit protects the Church, and especially the successor of the Apostles, from dogmatic and moral error. That is true. But it is also much more important to realize that the Holy Spirit is given to each member of the Church to guide him in the truth, to lead him to his supernatural destination, and to open his eyes to the mystery of God's presence and action in his own life.

In the discourse at the Last Supper, the Savior Who was about to die on the Cross returned insistently to the theme of His departure from His disciples in His physical and material presence, in order to live in them mystically and spiritually by His Holy Spirit. But this is not to be understood as the mere substitution of metaphor for reality. Christ was not to be present in His members merely as a memory, as a model, as a good example. Nor would He merely guide and control them from afar, through angels. It is true that the Divine Nature infinitely transcends all that is natural, but in Christ the gap between God and man has been bridged by the Incarnation, and in us the gap is bridged by the invisible presence of the Holy Spirit. Christ is really present in us, more present than if He were standing before us visible to our bodily eyes. For we have become "other Christs."

By virtue of this hidden presence of the Spirit in our inmost self, we need only to deliver ourselves from preoccupation with our external, selfish, and illusory self in order to find God within us. And the Lord has explicitly said that this discovery, a sublime gift of His grace, normally implies some form of spiritual experience.

Christ says He will send us:

The Spirit of Truth whom the world cannot receive because it seeth Him not, nor knoweth Him: *but you shall know Him;* because He shall abide with you and he in you. (John 14:17)

The Holy Ghost, whom the Father will send in my name, *will teach you all things.* (John 14:26)

Through that Spirit the Father and the Son will both reveal themselves to us, and we will know and love them:

He that loveth me shall be loved of my Father: and *I will love him and will manifest myself to him.* . . . *My Father will love him and we will come to him and make our abode with him.* (John 14:21, 23)

But such knowledge and love, infused into our hearts by the God of love manifesting Himself to us, is essentially the same beatitude as the blessed enjoy in heaven. "For this is eternal life: That they may know Thee the only true God, and Jesus Christ whom Thou hast sent" (John 17:3).[9]

Eternal life is the *receiving* of the Lord sent by the Father, and of the Holy Spirit Who unites us to the Father in the Word. Eternal life is centered in these divine "sendings" or missions. Contemplation is the conscious, experiential awareness of the mission of the Son and of the Spirit, a reception of the Word Who is sent to us not only as life but also as light. But the full knowledge of the Word "sent" to us and "received" in us is subjective rather than objective. We know Him as the "other," as the divine "Thou" to Whom we turn the whole being of our spirit, and yet He is "in us" and is intimately united to our own inmost "I," so that He is more truly our self than we are.

Is it any wonder that this intimate knowledge of the Holy Trinity and of Jesus, the Incarnate Word, should open up infinite depths of joy and freedom to the contemplative Christian soul?

These things I have spoken to you *that my joy may be in you, and your joy may be filled.* (John 15:11)

Peace I leave with you, *my peace I give to you. Not as the world giveth do I give unto you* . . . (John 14:27)

The joy of the contemplative is consummated in perfect union:

The glory which Thou hast given to me I have given them; that they may be one as we also are one: I in them and Thou in me, that they may be made perfect in one. (John 17:22-23)

The seeds of this sublime life are planted in every Christian soul at Baptism.[10] But seeds must grow and develop before you reap the harvest. There are thousands of Christians walking about the face of the earth bearing in their bodies the infinite God of Whom they know practically nothing.[11] They are themselves sons of God and are not aware of their identity. Instead of seeking to know themselves and their true dignity, they struggle miserably to impersonate the alienated characters whose "greatness" rests on violence, craftiness, lust, and greed.

The seeds of contemplation and sanctity, planted in those souls, merely lie dormant. They do not germinate. They do not grow. In other words, sanctifying grace occupies the substance of their souls, but never flows out to inflame and irrigate and take possession of their faculties, their intellect and will. The presence of God never becomes an intimate reality. God does not manifest Himself to these souls because they do not seek Him with any real desire.

They are men divided between God and the world. They are at home only in their exterior self. They never seek what is deeper within them. They allow God to maintain His rights over the substance of their souls, but their thoughts and desires do not belong to Him. They belong to illusion, to passion, and to external things. Consequently, as far as their knowledge of God is concerned, these Christians are in the same condition as men without God. For them, too, the Spirit of Truth cannot fully be received "because they see Him not, nor know Him." For them too it must be said: "The sensual man perceiveth not these things that are of the Spirit of God: for it is foolishness to him and he cannot understand" (1 Corinthians 2:14).[12]

In His discourse at the Last Supper Jesus promised the Holy Ghost, with His contemplative gifts. But the promise was accompanied by a denial. The Holy Ghost would be given to those who would receive Him. To those who would not receive Him, He would be denied.

St. Thomas Aquinas, commenting on the words of St. John's Gospel (chap. 14), explains the difference between the two. Contemplation will be denied to a man in proportion as he belongs to "the world." The expression "the world" signifies those who love the transient and unimportant things of this world. They cannot receive the Holy Spirit Who is the Love of God. As St. John of the Cross says: "Two contraries cannot coexist at the same time in the same subject."[13] You cannot serve God and Mammon.

If a man wants to prepare himself to receive the Holy Ghost and His Love, he must withdraw his desires from all the ambitious, the external satisfactions and the temporal interests this world has to offer, for spiritual things cannot be appreciated or understood by the mind that is occupied with superficial[14] and merely external satisfactions. Spiritualia videri non possunt nisi quis vacet a terrenis.[15]

The Angelic Doctor explains that the Holy Ghost does not manifest Himself to worldly men because they do not desire to know

Him. They are content to occupy their minds with *trivial*[16] things. But desire is the most important thing in the contemplative life. Without desire we will never receive the great gifts of God. *Dona spiritualia non accipiuntur nisi desiderata.*[17] St. Thomas adds: *nec desiderantur nisi aliqualiter cognita.*[18] There could be no desire where there is not at least a little knowledge. We cannot desire union with God unless we know that such a union exists and have at least some idea of what it is.

But the *alienated*[19] man, and the Christian who is entirely concerned with external activities and temporal interests, not only does not desire contemplation, but he even makes himself incapable of knowing what it is. The only way to find out anything about the joys of contemplation is *by experience.* We must taste and see that the Lord is sweet. *Gustate et videte quoniam suavis est Dominus.*[20]

St. Thomas says that worldly men have lost that sense of taste for spiritual things. "As the tongue of a sick man cannot taste good things . . . so the soul infected with the corruption of the world has no taste for the joys of heaven."[21]

Sacred and Secular

Here we must pause a little to consider the difference between a *sacred* and a *secular* view of life. The expression "the world" is perhaps too vague. It does not merely refer to "what is all around us" or to the created universe. The universe is not evil, but good. The "world" in the bad sense certainly does not mean the cosmos, though in certain Christian Neoplatonist writings it tends to suggest that meaning. The *saeculum* is that which is temporal, which changes, revolves, and returns again to its starting point. This is due to Platonist and Gnostic influences which crept into Christianity and persuaded men that the universe was run by more or less fallen angels ("the powers of the air"). Our adjective "secular" comes from the Latin *saeculum,* which means both "world" and "century." The etymology of the word is uncertain. Perhaps it is related to the Greek *kuklon,* or "wheel," from which we get "cycle." So originally, that which is "secular" is that which goes around in interminably recurring cycles. That is what "worldly society" does. Its horizons are those of an ever recurring sameness:

> One generation passeth away and another generation cometh: but the earth standeth forever. The sun also riseth and goeth down and returneth to his place: and there rising again maketh his round by the south and turneth again to the north: the spirit goeth forward surveying all places round about and returneth to his circuits. . . . What is it that hath been? The same thing that shall be. What is it that hath been done? The same that shall be done. Nothing under the sun is new. . . . Vanity of vanities, and all is vanity. (Ecclesiastes 1)

Now all our existence in this life is subject to change and recurrence. That alone does not make it secular. But life becomes secularized when it commits itself completely to the "cycles" of what *appears to be new,* but is in fact the same thing over again. Secular life is a life of vain hopes imprisoned in the illusion of newness and change, an illusion which brings us constantly back to the same old point, the contemplation of our own nothingness. Secular life is a life frantically dedicated to escape, through novelty and variety, from the fear of death. But the more we cherish secular hopes, the more they disappoint us. And the more they disappoint us, the more desperately do we return to the attack and forge new hopes more extravagant than the last. These too let us down. And we revert to that insufferable condition from which we have vainly tried to escape. In the words of Pascal:[22]

> Nothing is so unbearable to a man as to be completely at rest, without passions, without business, without diversion, without study. He then feels his nothingness, his falseness, his insufficiency, his dependence, his weakness, his emptiness . . . (*Pensées,* 131)

"Secular" society is by its nature committed to what Pascal calls "diversion," that is, to movement which has, before everything else, the anesthetic function of quieting our anguish. All society, without exception, tends to be in some respect "secular." But a genuinely secular society is one which cannot be content with innocent escapes from itself. More and more it tends to need and to demand, with insatiable dependence, satisfaction in pursuits that are unjust, evil, or even criminal. Hence the growth of economically useless businesses that exist for profit and not for real production, that create artificial needs which they then fill with cheap and quickly exhausted products. Hence the wars that arise when producers compete for markets and sources of raw material. Hence the nihilism, despair, and destructive anarchy that follow war, and then the blind rush into totalitarianism as an escape from despair. Our world has now reached the point when, for the sake of diversion, it is ready to blow itself up. The atomic age is the highest point ever achieved by secularism. And this reminds us, of course, that the real root of secularism is godlessness.

The secular and sacred reflect two kinds of dependence. The secular world depends upon the things it needs to divert itself and escape from its own nothingness. It depends on the creation and multiplication of artificial needs, which it then pretends to "satisfy." Hence the secular world is a world that pretends to exalt man's liberty, but in which man is in fact enslaved by the things on which he depends. In secular society man himself is alienated and becomes a "thing" rather than a person, because he is subject to the rule of what is lower than himself and outside himself. He is subject to his ever increasing needs, to his restlessness, his dissatisfaction, his anxiety, and his fear, but above all to the guilt which reproaches him for infidelity to his own inner truth. To escape this guilt, he plunges further into falsity.

In the sacred society, on the other hand, man admits no dependence on anything lower than himself, or even "outside" himself in a spatial sense. His only Master is God. Only when God is our Master can we be free, for God is within ourselves as well as above us. He rules us by liberating us and raising us to union with Himself *from within*. And in so doing He liberates us from our dependence on created things outside us. We use and dominate them, so that they exist for our sakes, and not we for theirs. There is no purely sacred society except in heaven.

But the city of God in heaven is reflected on earth in the society of those who are united not by "enlightened self-interest," but by sacrificial and Christian love, by mercy and compassion, by selfless and divine pity.

They liberate themselves from slavery to "diversion" by renouncing their own pleasure and immediate satisfaction in order to help relieve the needs of others, and in order to help others in turn to become free and to seek their own inner truth and thus fulfill their destiny on earth.

I have said that even the most sacred of earthly societies tends to have something of a secular character. This is inevitable as soon as we have a visible society of men in the present fallen condition of human nature. The visible and symbolic expressions of the divine tend to become opaque in their constant use by men, so that we stop at them and no longer go through them to God. Hence Holy Communion, for instance, tends to become a routine and "secularized" activity when it is sought not so much as a mystical contact with the Incarnate Word of God and with all the members of His Mystical Body, but rather as a way of gaining social approval and allaying feelings of anxiety. In this manner even the most sacred realities can be debased and, without totally losing their sacred character, enter into the round of secular "diversion."

The truly sacred attitude toward life is in no sense an escape from the sense of nothingness that assails us when we are left alone with ourselves. On the contrary, it penetrates into that darkness and that nothingness, realizing that the mercy of God has transformed our nothingness into His temple and believing that in our darkness His light has hidden itself. Hence the sacred attitude is one which does not recoil from our own inner emptiness, but rather penetrates into it with awe and reverence, and with the awareness of mystery.

This is a most important discovery in the interior life. For the external self *fears* and recoils from what is beyond it and above it. It dreads the seeming emptiness and darkness of the interior self. The whole tragedy of "diversion" is precisely that it is a flight from all that is most real and immediate and genuine in ourselves. It is a flight from life and from experience—an attempt to put a veil of objects between the mind and its experience of itself. It is therefore a matter of great courage and spiritual energy to turn away from diversion and prepare to meet, face-to-face, that *immediate* experience of life which is intolerable to the exterior man. This is only possible when, by a gift of God (St. Thomas would say it was the Gift of Fear, or sacred awe) we are able to see our inner selves not as a vacuum but as an *infinite depth,* not as emptiness but as fullness. This change of perspective is impossible as long as we are afraid of our own nothingness, as long as we are afraid of fear, afraid of poverty, afraid of boredom—as long as we run away from ourselves.

What we need is the gift of God which makes us able to find in ourselves not just ourselves, but Him: and then our nothingness becomes His all. This is not possible without the liberation effected by communication and humility. It requires not talent, not mere insight, but *sorrow,* pouring itself out in *love* and *trust.*

The sacred attitude is essentially contemplative, and the secular attitude essentially active. That does not mean that there cannot be an activity that is sacred (based on love). But even such activity is sacred only insofar as it tends to contemplation.

The man whose view of life is purely secular hates himself interiorly, while seeming to love himself. He hates himself in the sense that he cannot stand to be "with" or "by" himself. And because he hates himself, he also tends to hate God, because he cannot abide the inner loneliness which must be suffered and accepted before God can be found. His rebellion against his own inner loneliness and poverty turns into pride. Pride is the fixation of the exterior self upon itself and the rejection of all other elements in the self for which it is incapable of assuming responsibility. This includes the rejection of the inmost self, with its apparent emptiness, its indefiniteness, and its general character as that which is dark and unknown. Pride is, then, a false and evasive self-realization which is in actual fact no realization at all, but only the fabrication of an illusory image. The effort which must then be put into the protection and substantiation of this illusion gives an appearance of strength. But in reality, this fixation upon what does not exist merely exhausts and ruins our being.

There is a subtle but inescapable connection between the "sacred" attitude and the acceptance of one's inmost self. The movement of recognition which accepts our own obscure and unknown self produces the sensation of a "numinous" presence within us. This sacred awe is no mere magic illusion, but the real expression of a release of spiritual energy, testifying to our own interior reunion and reconciliation with that which is deepest in us and, through the inner self, with the transcendent and invisible power of God. This implies humility, or the full acceptance of all that we have tended to reject and ignore in ourselves. The inner self is "purified" by the acknowledgment of sin, not precisely because the inner self is the seat of sin, but because both our sinfulness and our interiority tend to be rejected in one and the same movement by the exterior self and relegated to the same darkness, so that when the inner self is brought back to light, sin emerges and is liquidated by the assuming of responsibility and by sorrow.

Thus the man with the "sacred" view is one who does not need to hate himself, and is never afraid or ashamed to remain with his own loneliness, for in it he is at peace, and through it he can come to the presence of God. More still, he is able to go out from his own loneliness to find God in other men. That is to say, in his dealings with others he has no need to identify them with their sins and condemn them for their actions, for he is able, in them also, to see below the surface and to guess at the presence of the inner and innocent self that is the image of God. Such a man is able to help other men to find God in themselves, educating them in confidence by the respect he is able to feel for them. Thus he is capable of allaying some of their fears and helping them to put up with themselves, until they become interiorly quiet and *learn*[23] to see God in the depths of their own poverty.

The basic and most fundamental problem of the spiritual life is this acceptance of our hidden and dark self, with which we tend to identify all the evil that is in us. We must learn by discernment to separate the evil growth of our actions from the good ground of the soul. And we must prepare that ground so that a new life can grow up from it within us, beyond our knowledge and beyond our conscious control. The sacred attitude is, then, one of reverence, awe, and silence before the mystery that begins to take place within us when we become aware of our inmost self. In silence, hope, expectation, and unknowing, the man of faith abandons himself to the divine will: not as to an arbitrary and magic power whose decrees must be spelled out from cryptic ciphers, but as to the stream of reality and of life itself. The sacred attitude is, then, one of deep and fundamental respect for the real in whatever new form it may present itself.

The secular attitude is one of gross disrespect for reality, upon which the worldly mind seeks only to force its own crude patterns. The secular man is the slave of his own prejudices, preconceptions, and limitations. The man of faith is ideally free from prejudice and plastic in his uninhibited response to each new movement of the stream of life. I say "ideally" in order to exclude those whose faith is not pure but is also another form of prejudice enthroned in the exterior man—a preconceived opinion rather than a living responsiveness to the *logos* of each new situation. For there exists a kind of "hard" and rigid religious faith that is not really alive or spiritual, but resides entirely in the exterior self and is the product of conventionalism and systematic prejudice. Speaking of the obedience and docility of the man of faith, Christ made clear that this union with the will of God in action is the necessary step to contemplative awareness of God:

> *If you love me* ... I will ask the Father and He will give you another Paraclete.... *He that loveth me shall* be loved of my Father and *I will love him and manifest myself to him.* (John 14:15–16, 21)

And He added the final, perfect test, the proof of true love and the one decisive factor which distinguishes the contemplative from the man of the world, the saint from the mediocre Christian. *"If anyone love me he will keep my word.* ... *He that loveth me not keepeth not my words"* (John 14:23–24).

It is really this total and uncompromising docility to the will of God that gives a man a taste for spiritual things. It is this delicate instinct to yield to the slightest movement of God's love that makes the true contemplative. As St. Thomas says: *Per obedientiam homo efficitur idoneus ad videndum Deum.* "It is obedience that makes a man fit to see God."[24]

[FIVE]

Kinds of Contemplation

Strictly speaking, contemplation is an immediate and in some sense passive intuition of the inmost reality, of our spiritual self and of God present within us.[1] But there is also an active and mediate form of contemplation in which this perception is attained in some measure by our own efforts, though with the mysterious and invisible help of grace. The concept of passive or infused contemplation is primarily theological. That is to say, it refers to a reality which is not directly or empirically verifiable, but which is a datum of revelation. This should not be made to sound more mysterious or esoteric than it really is. The revelation of this "passive" intuition seems to be implicit in the statements from St. John's Gospel that have just been quoted. When Christ says, "I will manifest myself to him," it means that the "activity" is on the side of the Lord, and that the one who contemplates the divine presence is in no position to bring about its manifestation by any effort of his own. Nor is he capable of increasing or modifying it by his efforts. And even, in some cases, he is incapable of *preventing* it. The classical expression for such a grace as this is that it is effected in us and without us: *In nobis et sine nobis.* Active or mediate contemplation, on the other hand, is effected in us but with our own active cooperation: *In nobis et non sine nobis.*

Normally, a life of active contemplation prepares a man for occasional and unpredictable visits of infused or passive contemplation. Also, active contemplation can never attain the depth and the purity of infused contemplation, which, in its purest form, takes place entirely without conceptual mediation. In active contemplation concept and judgment, or at least acts of faith springing from a certain mental activity, serve as a springboard for contemplative intuitions and for states of quietude more or less prolonged.

In active contemplation, there is a deliberate and sustained effort to detect the will of God in events and to bring one's whole self into harmony with that will. Active contemplation depends on ascesis of abandonment, a systematic relaxation of the tensions of the exterior self and a renunciation of its tyrannical claims and demands, in order to move in a dimension that escapes our understanding and overflows in all directions our capacity to plan. The element of dialectic in active contemplation is centered on the discovery of God's will, that is to say, the identification of the real direction which events are taking, especially in our own life. But along with this there is a deep concern with the symbolic and ritual enactment of those sacred mysteries which *represent*[2] the divine actions by which the redemption and sanctification of the world is *effected*.[3] In other words, active contemplation rests on a deep ground of liturgical, historical, and cultural tradition: but a living tradition, not dead convention. And a tradition still in dynamic movement and growth.

The contemplative mind is, in fact, not normally ultraconservative, but neither is it necessarily radical. It transcends both these extremes in order to remain in living contact with that which is genuinely true in any traditional movement. Hence I would say in parentheses that the contemplative mind today will not normally be associated too firmly or too definitively with any "movement," whether political, religious, liturgical, artistic, philosophical, or what have you. The contemplative stays clear of movements, not because they confuse him, but simply because he does not need them and can go farther by himself than he can in their formalized and often fanatical ranks.

Nevertheless active contemplation should be to a great extent in contact with the *logos* of its age. Which means in simple fact that the contemplative today might be expected to have an intuitive grasp of and even sympathy for what is most genuine in the characteristic movements of our time—Marxism, existentialism, psychoanalysis, eirenism. They may even at times present a serious temptation for him. But if he is a genuine contemplative, he will be able to resist temptation because his contemplation itself will instinctively avoid becoming enmeshed in conceptual systems. I say if he is a genuine contemplative, meaning "if he is sufficiently initiated into the meaning and value of a spiritual life to prefer its simplicity to all the complexities and pretenses of these intellectual fads and campaigns."

In active contemplation, a man becomes able to live within himself. He learns to be at home with his own thoughts. He becomes to a greater and greater degree independent of exterior supports. His mind is pacified not by passive dependence on things outside himself—diversions, entertainments, conversations, business—but by its own constructive activity. That is to say, that he derives inner satisfaction from spiritual creativeness: thinking his own thoughts, reaching his own conclusions, looking at his own life and directing it in accordance with his own inner truth, discovered in meditation and under the eyes of God. He derives strength not from what he gets out of things and people, but *from*[4] giving himself to life and to others. He discovers the secret of life in the *creative energy of love*—not love as a sentimental or sensual indulgence, but as a profound and self-oblative expression of freedom.

Active contemplation is nourished by meditation and reading and, as we shall see, by the sacramental and liturgical life of the Church. But before reading, meditation, and worship turn into contemplation, they must merge into a *unified and intuitive vision* of reality.

In reading, for instance, we pass from one thought to another, we follow the development of the author's ideas, and we contribute some ideas of our own if we read well. This activity is discursive. Reading becomes contemplative when, instead of reasoning, we abandon the sequence of the author's thoughts in order not only to follow our own thoughts (meditation), but simply *to rise above thought and penetrate into the mystery of truth which is experienced intuitively as present and actual*. We meditate with our mind, which is "part of" our being. But we contemplate with our whole being and not just with one of its parts.

This means that the contemplative intuition of reality is a perception of value: a perception which is not intellectual or speculative, but practical and experiential. It is not just a matter of observation, but of realization. It is not something abstract and general, but concrete and particular. It is a personal grasp of the existential meaning and value of reality.

Such personal intuitions may be highly paradoxical and even, sometimes, disturbing. The sense of experiential awareness is very strong, yet there is no discursive intellectual evidence to support this awareness. Hence a peculiar combination of certainty and hazard. One "knows" without knowing how he knows. And this of course can be quite dangerous. It can lead to illusion and to illuminism. The contemplative's only safeguard is humility and self-forgetfulness and the renunciation of all desire to exploit the experience for any purpose whatever. What happens, happens. One accepts it, in humility, and sees it, without inferring anything or instituting any comparison with other experiences. And one walks on in the presence of God. Rightly accepted, contemplative experience has its own proper effect: it increases the intensity and simplicity of a man's love for God and for his fellow men. If it could be said to have a "purpose," then this would be its purpose. But in reality contemplation has no purpose outside itself for, properly understood, it is inseparably joined to love and identified with love. The love which is essential to contemplation is its "purpose" as well as its source. It needs no other.

The beauty of truth seen by the intelligence draws our hearts out of themselves in love and admiration. When the work of thought leads to an intuition of love and of religious awe, then we have "active contemplation."

The religious element in contemplation must be stressed here. There exists also a nonreligious and aesthetic contemplation—a kind of aesthetic complacency in the beauty of abstract truth. But unless the note of sacred awe heightens the perception of intellectual beauty, we do not yet have contemplation in the religious sense of the word. And here perhaps we must recognize the limitations and deficiencies of the term. The word "contemplation" is too pale, too vague, and too inactive to convey the full spiritual strength of a genuinely religious experience of God. If we are to continue using the word at all, we must strengthen it, forget its purely pagan and intellectual connotations, and think rather of the trembling with which Moses "loosed the shoes from off his feet" on Mount Horeb when

God spoke to him out of the burning bush and warned him that he stood upon holy ground. Contemplation, in the Christian context, necessarily implies a sacred "dread"—a holy awe.

Liturgy

Active contemplation is not the mere perception and enjoyment of an abstract spiritual truth. It is a participation in the Church's collective experience in receiving, from God, the concrete revelation of His divine mystery. Hence the liturgy is the ordinary focus of active contemplation. In the sacred liturgy we have, of course, symbolic rites and ceremonies, music, speech, poetry, collective prayer. But to pass through liturgy into contemplation is something much more than mere aesthetic enjoyment of a religious concert or of a very primitive form of sacred drama.

The Christian liturgy is contemplative on two levels: on the level of *spoken revelation* and on the level of *ritual mystery,* or *sacred action.* On the level of spoken revelation we have the chanting, or at least reading of sacred texts containing not only moral truths and ascetic counsels, but much more, the *formal announcement (kerygma)* of the *evangelium,* the mystery of man's salvation. When we stand to listen to the Gospel, we formally and solemnly bear witness to our faith, and by that faith receive into our hearts the very substance of the truth which God reveals to us. We receive the "word of salvation," which is "sharper than any two-edged sword,"[5] which enters into the depths of our being with a supernatural and transforming power, and which awakens or renews in us our divine life as sons of God. To be aware of this inner reality, as the result of our attentive and loving faith, and to "realize" the truth of God's love for us and for the world is to enter into the way of "active contemplation" which the liturgy lays open to us.

Certain[6] moments in the liturgy of solemn fast days (like the Ember days) remind us of this interconnection between public revelation and private contemplation. At the end of certain scriptural texts the Deacon sings *Flectamus genua* ("Let us kneel down"), and this is, or should be, followed by a few minutes of silent prayer in which each one supposedly enters into the full *awareness*[7] of the words that have just been sung. Unfortunately this practice long ago lost its original meaning, and it is only just beginning to come back into liturgical use.

The higher level of liturgical contemplation is in *sacred action,* the ritual of the sacraments and above all of the great mystery, the Holy Eucharist. These rites and divine gifts are more than symbols; they contain the very realities which their symbolism expresses and bring with them graces to illuminate the eyes of the heart to perceive their inner meaning. Indeed, the sacrament of Baptism was known in ancient times as an "illumination" (*photismos*), and the ritual of this sacrament of Christian initiation still tells us eloquently that it brings not only faith, but the power to taste the fullness of faith in contemplation.

Not only does the Church pray God to illuminate the mind of the candidate and drive all blindness from his *inmost*[8] heart, but all his senses are signed with chrism that he may hear the precepts of God, see the brightness of God, smell the sweet odor of Christ, speak the words of life, and believe in the word of the Lord. The whole being of the baptized Christian is signed in the name of the Holy Trinity, and the mystical senses are awakened in him by the grace of the sacrament. *Baptism sanctifies us by bringing to life our inmost self as a "new man in Christ."*[9] At that time *one*[10] receives the seven Gifts of the Holy Ghost, which, according to the teaching of St. Thomas, are spiritual faculties making possible a full mystical life in anyone who completely renounces the world and yields himself completely to the action of God.

But Baptism is only the beginning of the noble and sublime existence of the Christian as son of God. The greatest of the sacraments and the one which perfects and completes all the others is the Blessed Eucharist, the mystery of Christ's love, in which the Christian is sacramentally united to the Risen Lord in Holy Communion. Receiving the Sacred Body of the Savior in the consecrated Host, the believer affirms his union with Christ in His Passion, Death, and Resurrection from the Dead. He becomes one heart, one mind, and one spirit with the Blessed Savior. He becomes lost in the Mystical Christ as a drop of water becomes lost in a chalice of wine. The mystery of the Eucharist both symbolizes and effects the mystical union of the believer with Christ by charity. The grace of contemplation enables him to penetrate into the full meaning of this mystery, to realize its depths and its extent. Contemplation is but a weak word for the great gift which St. Paul calls the "spirit of wisdom and revelation in the knowledge of Christ," which leaves us with

> The eyes of the heart enlightened . . . to know the riches of the glory of His inheritance. . . . To know also the charity of Christ which surpasses all understanding and to be filled unto all the fullness of God. (Ephesians 1, 3)

By active participation in the liturgy the Christian prepares himself to enter into the Church's "contemplation" of the great mysteries of faith. Here, least of all, is contemplation something merely mental and discursive. It involves man's whole being, body and soul, mind, will, imagination, emotion, and spirit. Worship takes man in his wholeness and consecrates him *entirely*[11] to God, and thence contemplation is the perfection of worship. Without contemplation worship tends to remain lifeless and external. The mere existence of the Church's liturgy is, then, a call to active contemplation. To remain withdrawn from the liturgy and outside it is to exclude oneself from possibilities of active contemplation that the Church offers to all, with many graces and lights that she alone is privileged to distribute to her children.

At the Last Supper, Jesus gave us more than a sublime doctrine: He gave us Himself, "the way, the truth and the life." The Blessed Sacrament is not a sign or a figure of contemplation; it contains Him Who is the beginning and end of all contemplation. It should not be surprising, then, that one of the most normal ways of entering into infused prayer is through the graces given in Holy Communion.

Union with God in Activity

The great majority of Christians will never become pure contemplatives on earth. But that does not mean that those whose vocation is essentially active must resign themselves to being excluded from all the graces of a deep interior life and all infused prayer. Christ has promised that the Three Divine Persons will manifest themselves *to all who love Him*. There are many Christians who serve God with great purity of soul and perfect self-sacrifice in the active life. Their vocation does not allow them to find the solitude and silence and leisure in which to empty minds entirely of created things and to lose themselves in God alone. They are too busy serving Him in His children on earth. At the same time, their minds and temperaments do not fit them for a purely contemplative life: they would know no peace without exterior activity. They would not know what to do with themselves. They would vegetate, and *their interior life would grow cold.*

Nevertheless, they know how to find God by devoting themselves to Him in self-sacrificing labors in which they are able to remain in His presence all day long. They live and work in His company. They realize that He is within them, and they taste deep, peaceful joy in being with Him. They lead lives of great simplicity in which they do not need to rise above the ordinary levels of vocal and affective prayer. Without realizing it, their *extremely simple*[12] prayer is, for them, so deep and interior that it brings them to the threshold of contemplation. They never enter deeply into the contemplative life, but they are not unfamiliar with graces akin to contemplation. Although they are active laborers, they are also *hidden contemplatives*[13] because of the great purity of heart maintained in them by obedience, fraternal charity, self-sacrifice, and perfect abandonment to God's will in all that they do and suffer. They are much closer to God than they realize. They enjoy a kind of "masked" contemplation.[14]

Such Christians as these, far from being excluded from perfection, may reach a higher degree of sanctity than others who have been apparently favored with a deeper interior life. Yet there is all the difference in the world between these hidden contemplatives and the surface Christian whose piety is merely a matter of externals and formal routine. The difference is: *these men live for God and for His love alone.* They cannot help knowing something about Him.[15]

It might be well to point out here that "masked contemplation" has its advantages. Since contemplation is communion with a hidden God in His own hiddenness, it tends to be pure in proportion as it is itself hidden. Obscurity and sincerity seem to go together in the spiritual life. The "masked contemplative" is one whose contemplation is hidden from no one so much as from himself. This may seem like a contradiction in terms. Yet it is a strange and deep truth that the grace of contemplation is most secure and most efficacious when it is no longer sought, or cherished, or desired. It is in a sense most pure when it is barely known. Of course, for it to be contemplation at all, there must be some awareness of it. If there is absolutely no awareness, then there is no contemplation.

Here we speak of an awareness that is present, but utterly unself-conscious. It is a kind of negative awareness, an "unknowing." According to the classical expression of Pseudo-Dionysius,[16] one knows God by "not-knowing" Him. One reaches Him "apophatically" in the darkness beyond concepts. And one contemplates, so to speak, by forgetting that one is able to contemplate. As soon as one is aware of himself contemplating, the gift is spoiled. This was long ago observed by St. Anthony of the Desert,[17] who said: "That prayer is most pure in which the monk is no longer aware of himself, or of the fact that he is praying."

Often people think that this remark of St. Anthony refers to some curious state of psychological absorption, a kind of mystical sleep. In point of fact, it refers to a selfless awareness, a spiritual liberty and lightness and freedom which transcends all special psychological states and is "no state" at all. Would-be contemplatives must be on their guard against a kind of heavy, inert stupor in which the mind becomes swallowed up in itself. To remain immersed in one's own darkness is not contemplation, and no one should attempt to "stop" the functioning of his mind and remain fixed on his own nothingness. Rather, we must go out in hope and faith from our own nothingness and seek liberation in God.

The masked contemplative is liberated from *temporal*[18] concern by his own purity of intention. He no longer seeks himself in action or in prayer, and he has achieved a kind of holy indifference, abandoning himself to the will of God and seeking only to keep in touch with the realities of the present moment. By this of course I mean the inner and spiritual realities, not the surface emotions and excitements which are not reality but illusion.

The life of contemplation in action and purity of heart is, then, a life of great simplicity and inner liberty. One is not seeking anything special or demanding any particular satisfaction. One is content with what is. One does what is to be done, and the more concrete it is, the better. One is not worried about the results of what is done. One is content to have good motives and not too anxious about making mistakes. In this way one can swim with the living stream of life and remain at every moment in contact with God, in the hiddenness and ordinariness of the present moment with its obvious task.

At such times, walking *down*[19] a street, sweeping a floor, washing dishes, hoeing beans, reading a book, taking a stroll in the woods—all can be enriched with contemplation and with the obscure sense of the presence of God. This contemplation is all the more pure in that one does not "look" to see if it is there. Such "walking with God" is one of the simplest and most secure ways of living a life of prayer, and one of the safest. It never attracts anybody's attention, least of all the attention of him who lives it. And he soon learns *not to want to see* anything special in himself. This is the price of his liberty.

It has been said above that such people enjoy "graces akin to contemplation" because they are never fully conscious of their "contemplative state." But it must not be thought that they cannot be real mystics. Indeed, a genuine mystical life may be lived in these conditions. The mystical graces given to such souls may be of an active character, but there is a strong undercurrent of contemplative intuition. This will remain pure and vital as long as one is careful not to lose himself in activity, not to become preoccupied with results, and not to lose his purity of intention. Whether in active or passive contemplation, purity of heart is always the guardian of contemplative truth.

Acquired and Infused Contemplation

So far we have deliberately avoided a classification that divides contemplation into "acquired" and "infused," because the legitimacy of this division has been hotly contested by theologians, and there seems to be little point in resurrecting a controversy which has by now died a natural death. This battle raged, somewhat *fruitlessly*,[20] throughout the twenties and thirties of our [the twentieth] century. The contestants were trying to determine what were the phenomenological limits of mystical prayer: when did a state of prayer cease to be "natural" or "acquired" and become "supernatural" or "infused"? In other words, when did man cease to be himself the principal agent and yield this primacy to the Spirit of God? At what point does prayer show signs of being truly "mystical"? The other question involved in this was: is it possible by certain sustained efforts, inspired by the grace of God, to prepare oneself for and to enter into genuine contemplation?

The questions, which soon became complex, seem to be, in perspective, rather nugatory disputes about words. In particular everything depended on the way one defined "contemplation" and "mystical." Those who divided contemplation into "natural" and "supernatural" said that (natural) contemplation could be acquired. This natural and acquired contemplation was something like what has been described in these pages as active contemplation: an intuitive perception of supersensory reality, reached after preliminary spiritual efforts of the contemplative himself. But the defenders of acquired contemplation held that this contemplation was not really mystical.

Others, speaking evidently of the same state of prayer, held that it was true and mystical contemplation, but that it was not acquired. It was a *passive*[21] supernatural gift.

Natural Contemplation and Mystical Theology

In these pages, I have decided to ignore the complexities of this now defunct argument, and have simply assumed the existence of a supersensory intuition of the divine which is a gift of grace for which we can, to some extent, prepare ourselves by our own efforts. In this I am basing myself on a distinction made by the Greek Fathers: that between natural contemplation (*theoria physike*) and theology (*theologia*), or the contemplation of God.

Theoria physike is the intuition of divine things in and through the reflection of God in nature and in the symbols of revelation. It presupposes a complete purification of heart by a long ascetic preparation which has delivered the soul from subjection to passion and, consequently, from the illusions generated by passionate attachment to *exterior*[22] things. When the eye is clear and "single" (that is to say, disinterested—having only "one intention"), then it can see things as they are. The contemplative at this stage is one whose thoughts are no longer passionate, no longer distorted. They are simple and direct. He sees straight into the nature of things as they are. At the same time he sees into his own nature. And this is a mystical grace from God.

Now the word "natural" in connection with this kind of contemplation refers not to its origin, but to its object. *Theoria physike* is contemplation of the divine *in nature,* not contemplation of the divine *by our natural powers.* And in fact, "natural contemplation" in this sense is mystical: that is to say, it is a gift of God, a divine enlightenment. But it still involves labor and preparation on the part of the contemplative. He has to look about him, see the created world and the symbols with which it is filled. *He has to*[23] receive, in the sign language of Scripture and liturgy, words of God which transform his inner life. Natural contemplation, according to the Greek Fathers, also "sees" and communes with the angelic beings who form a part of created nature. This natural contemplation, which beholds the divine in and through nature, has served me as a prototype for what I have chosen to call "active contemplation"—a contemplation which man seeks and prepares by his own initiative but which, by a gift of God, *is completed in mystical intuition.*[24]

Theologia, or pure contemplation ("mystical theology" in the language of Pseudo Denis [Pseudo-Dionysius]), is a direct quasi-experiential contact with God beyond all thought, that is to say, without the medium of concepts. This excludes not only concepts tinged with passion, or sentimentality, or imagination, but even the simplest intellectual intuitions that require some sort of medium between God and the spirit. Theology in this sense is a direct contact with God. Now this supreme Christian contemplation, according to the Greek Fathers, is a quasi-experiential knowledge of God as He is in Himself, that is to say, of God as Three Persons in One Nature: for this is the highest mystery in which He has revealed Himself to us.

Entrance into this supreme mystery is not a matter of spiritual effort, of intellectual subtlety, still less of learning. It is a matter of identification by charity, for charity is the likeness of the soul to God. As St. John says:

> Everyone that loveth is born of God, and knoweth God. He that loveth not, knoweth not God, for God is charity. . . . In this we know that we abide in Him and He in us, because He hath given us of His Spirit. And we have seen and do testify that the Father hath sent His Son to be the Savior of the world. (1 John 4:7–8, 13–14)

This apparently simple text of the Apostle contains in it immense depths of theology: it gives the full justification of the teaching of the Christian mystics on the possibility of our apprehending, in contemplative charity, the very being of God as He is in Himself. For the man who is perfect in love becomes like God Who is Love, and in this he is able to experience within himself the presence of the Three Divine Persons, the Father, the source and giver of Love, the Son, the image and glory of Love, and the Spirit Who is the communication of the Father and the Son in Love.

But this theology has one other characteristic that must not be over-looked. It is a contact with God in charity, yes, but also and above all in the darkness of unknowing. This follows necessarily from the fact that it goes beyond the symbols and intuitions of the intellect, and attains to God directly without the medium of any created image. If a medium there is, it is not intellectual, not an image or species in the mind, but a disposition of our whole being, brought about by that love which so likens and conforms us to God that we become able to experience Him mystically in and through *our inmost*[25] selves, as if He were our very selves. The *inner*[26] self of the mystic, elevated and transformed in Christ, united to the Father in the Son, through the Holy Spirit, now knows God not so much through the medium of an objective image as through its own divinized subjectivity. Truly a difficult thing to convey in words, and still more difficult to imagine, if one has not experienced it. The best we can do is read and meditate on the texts of the masters who are able to speak from experience. Here, for instance, is St. Gregory of Nyssa[27] interpreting in this sense the symbolism of Moses' ascent of Sinai into the dark cloud where he is face-to-face with God. We remember that the "animals and human beings" must be kept away from the foot of the mountain. They must not even touch it, under pain of death. This, says Gregory, suggests the fact that passionate and even simple concepts must be kept away from the mountain of contemplation. The spirit must ascend into the darkness *without any concept at all*.

> The more the spirit in its forward progress arrives, by ever greater and more perfect application, at an understanding of what it means to know these realities, and comes closer and closer to contemplation, the more it sees that the divine nature is invisible. Having left behind all appearances, not only those which are perceived by the senses, but also those which the intelligence believes itself to apprehend, it enters further and further within until, with great struggle of the spirit, it penetrates to the Invisible and Unknowable, and there sees God. (*De Vita Moysi*, ii, 162; *Sources Chrétiennes*)

Now this "vision" of God is a vision in darkness, and therefore is not the face-to-face vision enjoyed by the Blessed in Paradise. Yet it is an equally real and genuine contact with God, the chief distinction being that it takes place without clarity and without "seeing." In fact, the spirit sees God precisely by understanding that He is utterly invisible to it. In this sudden, deep, and total acceptance of his invisibility, it casts far from itself every last trace of conceptual mediation, and in so doing rids itself of the spiritual obstacles which stand between it and God. Thoughts, *natural*[28] light, and spiritual images are, so to speak, veils or coverings that impede the direct, naked sensitivity by which the spirit touches the Divine Being. When the veils are removed, then one can touch, or rather be touched by, God in the mystical darkness. Intuition reaches Him by one final leap beyond itself, an ecstasy in which it sacrifices itself and yields itself to His transcendent presence. In this last ecstatic act of "unknowing" the gap between our spirit as subject and God as object is finally closed, and in the embrace of mystical love we know that we and He are one. *This is infused or mystical contemplation in the purest sense of the term.*[29]

[SIX]

Infused Contemplation

In the loose and perhaps somewhat confusing description of contemplative experience on its different levels, we have seen that all forms of genuine contemplation have something in common.[1] Whether or not they are associated with our own efforts, they tend *toward*[2] an obscure, experiential contact with God beyond the senses and in some way even beyond concepts. Contemplation is pure in proportion as it is free from sensible and conceptual elements. The lower and more elementary mystical intuitions are those which are informed by and rely on symbols taken from the material world. The higher and more perfect contemplation goes beyond sense imagery and discursive understanding and flashes out in the darkness of "unknowing."

Perhaps the most important Patristic text on this subject is found in the opening lines of the *Mystical Theology* of Pseudo Denis the Areopagite [Pseudo-Dionysius]:

As far as is possible, raise thyself up in unknowing even unto union with Him Who is beyond all essence and all knowledge, for it is indeed by going out of thyself and out of all things with an irresistible leap, free and pure, that thou shalt raise thyself up to the pure and superessential ray of the divine darkness, after having abandoned all things and having liberated thyself from them all. . . . Then, delivered from all objects and from the very organs of contemplation (the contemplative) penetrates into the truly mystical Cloud of Unknowing in which he closes his eyes to all objects of knowledge and finds himself in utter intangibility and invisibility, since he now belongs entirely to Him Who is beyond all, and belongs no longer to any thing, neither to himself, nor to any other being, and is thus united in the most noble union with Him Who is utterly unknowable, by the cessation of all knowledge; in this total unknowing he now knows with a knowledge that is beyond understanding. (*Dictionnaire de Spiritualité,* ii, 1899)

It is to be noticed that Pseudo Denis, in this passage, insists on the contemplative's own activity in entering into the darkness of unknowing. However, he also stresses in the same chapter the concept which has had a decisive influence on all subsequent mystical thought. In the darkness of unknowing the contemplative passively receives the touch of divine knowledge (*Patitur divina*).[3] Traditionally, the most characteristic note of Christian contemplation is this passivity, this reception of divine light-in-darkness as a supremely mysterious and unaccountable gift of God's love.

We are now in a position to summarize the essential elements of mystical contemplation:

1. It is an intuition that on its lower level transcends the senses. On its higher level it transcends the intellect itself.

2. Hence it is characterized by a quality of light in darkness, knowing in unknowing. *It is beyond feeling, even beyond concepts.*[4]

3. In this contact with God, in darkness, there must be a certain activity of love on both sides. On the side of the soul, there must be a withdrawal from attachment to sensible things, a liberation of the mind and imagination from all strong emotional and passionate clinging to sensible realities. "Passionate thinking" distorts our intellectual vision, preventing us from seeing things as they are. But also, we must go beyond intelligence itself and not be attached even to "simple (*intuitive*)[5] thoughts." All thought, no matter how pure, is transcended in contemplation. The contemplative must, then, keep alert and detached from sensible and from even spiritual attachments. St. John of the Cross teaches us that the contemplative should turn away even from seemingly supernatural visions of God and of His saints in order to remain in the darkness of unknowing. In any event, con-

templation presupposes a generous and total effort of ascetic self-denial. But the *final ecstatic*[6] movement by which the contemplative "goes beyond" all things is passive and beyond his own control.

4. Contemplation is the work of love, and the contemplative proves his love by leaving all things, even the most spiritual things, for God in nothingness, detachment, and "night." But the deciding factor in contemplation is the free and unpredictable action of God. He alone can grant the gift of mystical grace and make Himself known by the secret, ineffable contact that reveals His presence in the depths of the soul. What counts is not the soul's love for God, but God's love for the soul.

5. This knowledge of God in unknowing is not intellectual, nor even in the strict sense affective. It is not the work of one faculty or another uniting the soul with an object outside itself. It is a work of interior union and of identification in divine charity. One knows God by becoming one with Him. One apprehends Him by becoming the object of His infinite mercies.

6. CONTEMPLATION IS A SUPERNATURAL LOVE AND KNOWLEDGE OF GOD, SIMPLE AND OBSCURE, INFUSED BY HIM INTO THE SUMMIT OF THE SOUL, GIVING IT A DIRECT AND EXPERIMENTAL CONTACT WITH HIM.[7]

Mystical contemplation is an intuition of God born of pure love. It is a gift of God that absolutely transcends all the natural capacities of the soul and which no man can acquire by any effort of his own. But God gives it to the soul in proportion as it is clean and emptied of all affections for things outside of Himself. In other words, it is God manifesting Himself, according to the promise of Christ, to those who love Him. Yet the love with which they love Him is also His gift; we only love Him because He has first loved us. We seek Him because He has already found us. *Ipse prior dilexit nos.*[8]

But the thing that must be stressed is that *contemplation is itself a development and a perfection of pure charity.* He who loves God realizes that the greatest joy, the perfection of beatitude is to love God and renounce all things for the sake of God alone—or for the sake of love alone because God Himself is love. Contemplation is an intellectual experience of the fact that God is infinite Love, that He has given Himself completely to us, and that henceforth love is all that matters.

7. St. Bernard[9] remarks that love is sufficient to itself, is its own end, its own merit, its own reward. It seeks no cause beyond itself and no fruit outside itself. The very act of loving is the greatest reward of love. To love with a pure, disinterested love the God Who is the source of all love can only be the purest and most perfect joy and the greatest of all rewards. *Amor praeter se non requirit causam, non fructum: fructus ejus, usus ejus.*[10] And he exclaims: "I love simply because I love, and I love in order to love." *Amo quia amo, amo ut amem (Sermon 83 in Cantica).*[11]

8. The experience of contemplative prayer, and the successive states of contemplation through which one passes, are all modified by the fact that the soul is passive, or partly passive, under the guidance of God. There is a special consolation in the sudden awareness and deep experiential conviction that one is being carried or led away by the love of God. But there is also a special anguish in the acute sense of one's own helplessness and dereliction, when one is powerless to do anything for himself. When our faculties can no longer serve us in their ordinary way, we are bound to pass through periods of strange incapacity, bitterness, and even apparent despair. In either case, it would be best not to pay too much attention to the "phenomenon" one seems to be experiencing. Better to purify one's intention and refrain from self-analysis. The *"depths"*[12] of dereliction and bitterness that *surround*[13] us when we are out of our natural *sphere*[14] do not lend themselves to accurate observation. At such times, reflection on ourselves too easily becomes morbid or hypochondriacal. Faith, patience, and obedience are the guides which must help us advance quietly in darkness without looking at ourselves.

As for the consolations of contemplative quietude: too intent a reflection on them quickly turns into a kind of narcissistic complacency and should be avoided. Even supposing that one is genuinely passive under the action of God (and some people are adept at imagining they are when this is not the case), still reflection on ourselves would be just the kind of activity that would prove an obstacle to the action of grace. The "ray of darkness" by which God enlightens our soul in passive contemplation has this about it: it makes us indifferent to ourselves, to our spiritual ambitions, and to our own "state." If we let the light of God play on the depth of our souls in its own way and refrain from too much curious self-inspection, we will gradually cease to worry about ourselves and forget these useless questions. This indifference and trust is itself a mystical grace, a gift of Divine Counsel, that leaves all decisions to God in the wordlessness of a present that knows no explanations, no projects, and no plans. *As Eckhart says, mystical love of God is a love that asks no questions.*[15]

9. Contemplation is the light of God playing directly upon the soul. But every soul is weakened and blinded by the attachment to created things, which it tends to love inordinately by reason of original sin. Consequently, the light of God affects that soul the way the light of the sun affects a diseased eye. It causes *pain.* God's love is too pure. The soul, impure and diseased, *weakened by its own*[16] selfishness, is shocked and repelled by the very purity of God. It cannot understand the suffering caused by the light of God. It has formed its own ideas of God: ideas that are based upon natural knowledge and which unconsciously flatter self-love. But God contradicts those ideas. His light *rejects*[17] and defeats all the natural notions the soul has formed for itself concerning Him. The experience of God in infused contemplation is a flat contradiction of all the soul has imagined about Him. The fire of His infused love *carries out*[18] a merciless attack upon the self-love of the soul attached to human consolations and to those lights and feelings which it required as a beginner, but which it falsely imagined to be the great graces of prayer.

10. Infused contemplation, then, sooner or later brings with it a terrible interior revolution. Gone is the sweetness of prayer. Meditation becomes impossible, even hateful. Liturgical functions seem to be an insupportable burden. The mind cannot think. The will seems unable to love. The interior life is filled with darkness and dryness and pain. The soul is tempted to think that all is over and that, in punishment for its infidelities, all spiritual life has come to an end.

This is a crucial point in the life of prayer. It is very often here that souls, called by God to contemplation, are repelled by this "hard saying," turn back, and "walk no more with Him" (John 6:61–67). God has illuminated their hearts with a ray of His light. But because they are blinded by its intensity, it proves to be, for them, a *ray of darkness*. They rebel against that. They do not want to *believe* and remain in obscurity: they want to *see*. They do not want to walk in emptiness, with blind trust: they want to know where they are going. They want to be able to depend on themselves. They want to trust their own minds and their own wills, their own judgments and their own decisions. They want to be their own guides. They are therefore sensual men who "do not perceive the things that are of the Spirit of God." To them, this darkness and helplessness is foolishness. Christ has given them His Cross and it has proved to be a scandal. They can go no further.

Generally they remain faithful to God: they try to serve Him. But they turn away from interior things and express their service in externals. They externalize themselves in pious practices, or they immerse themselves in work in order to escape the pain and sense of defeat they have experienced in what seems, to them, to be the collapse of all contemplation. *"The light shineth in darkness and the darkness did not comprehend it"* (John 1).[19]

11. This testing of the individual may perhaps be intensified by institutional circumstance. The anguish and fear which withdraw him from his precarious fidelity to inspirations that are purely interior spring from his conflict of standards. When one is called into the darkness of contemplation, he is called to leave familiar and conventional patterns of thought and action and to judge by an entirely new and hidden criterion: by the unseen light of the Holy Spirit. This of course is, from a certain point of view, fraught with great risk. How does one know that he is guided by God and not by the devil? How does one distinguish between grace and illusion?

The conflict is peculiarly delicate. Since, on the one hand, God definitely guides the contemplative by personal inspirations (at least in this matter of interior prayer), then the call to contemplation means a direct summons to leave the ordinary routine ways of the interior life and to live (or at least pray) by other standards—not the standards of books and manuals of piety, but the concrete inspirations of God here and now. But, on the other hand, one is not always under the guidance of God, and at the same time one remains a member of a more or less formalized social group, with objective norms of living to which one is bound to conform.

It can be said at once that the inspirations of the Holy Ghost[20] are seldom completely at variance with the *sanely traditional*[21] norms of religious societies. However, the history of the saints is full of examples when those led directly by God fell under the furious censure of professionally holy men. The trial of St. Joan of Arc is a case in point. The life of a contemplative is apt to be one constant tension and conflict between what he feels to be the interior movements of grace and the objective, exterior claims made upon him by the *society*[22] to whose laws he is subject. The tension is heightened by the realization that false mystics are always ready to claim exemption from social norms on the basis of private inspiration. And the *society*[23] itself, speaking through its most articulate members, will not be slow to remind him of the fact.

Even where the contemplative is not expressly forbidden to follow what he believes to be the inspiration of God (and this not rarely happens), he may feel himself continually and completely at odds with the accepted ideals of those around him. Their spiritual exercises may seem to him to be a bore and a waste of time. Their sermons and their conversation may leave him exhausted with a sense of futility: as if he had been pelted with words without meaning. Their choral offices, their excitement over liturgical ceremony and chant may rob him of the delicate taste of an interior manna that is not found in formulas of prayer and exterior rites. If only he could be alone and quiet, and remain in the emptiness, darkness, and purposelessness in which God speaks with such overwhelming effect! But no, *spiritual*[24] lights and nosegays are forced upon his mind, he must think and say words, he must sing "Alleluias" that somebody else wants him to feel. He must strive to smack his lips on a sweetness which seems to be unutterably coarse and foul: not because of what it aspires to say, but simply because it is secondhand.

I am told that among certain Near Eastern peoples it is a mark of honor, at a feast, for the host to give a guest a morsel which he himself has partly chewed. To a contemplative, life in a community dedicated to prayer gets to be this kind of a banquet all day long: you are always trying to swallow a dainty that has been chewed first by somebody else. The natural reaction is to spew it out of your mouth. But one does not dare, or if he does, he feels intolerable guilt.

This painful conflict would be more easily avoided if monastic institutions had not become so rigid and stereotyped in recent centuries, and if they had not to a great extent lost contact with the broad sanity of ancient tradition. Nothing is in fact so inimical to the contemplative life as regimentation. Rules are certainly necessary, and life under a monastic rule does not have to be a life of regimentation at all. Especially when all sane rules wisely foresee exceptions in individual cases and leave the superior to decide when a monk, by reason of his health, his employment, or *even his interior life,* requires the benefit of a more personal regime. It has, for instance, always been understood in oriental monasticism that in advancing years a monk might give himself more completely to contemplation and solitude. In this case he may live alone as a hermit or a recluse (witness the numerous cave-dwelling hermits on Mount Athos even today) or at least, in a *cenobium,* profit by longer hours of prayer. If it is foreseen that after a certain stage of one's spiritual development the Holy Ghost will take over and run one's life to suit Himself, then it is understandable that some latitude be left for His action. It is of course understood that *contumacy*[25] and *intractable willfulness*[26] clearly mark out a *man*[27] who is *not* guided by the Holy Spirit.

Unfortunately the modern tendency in the West has been to completely equate the "will of God" and the "action of the Holy Ghost" with the common and universal standard and to leave no place for the flowering of special graces in an individual. Wherever there is a conflict between the interior and the exterior, the exterior must always win. One must always, and above all, conform to the collective idea. Now it is true that this can be a very meritorious sacrifice, but it is equally true that short-sighted minds have turned the religious life, by this means, into a procrustean bed on which potential saints and contemplatives have been so pulled apart and crippled that they have ended their lives as freaks. And this is why, in so many contemplative monasteries, there are few or no real contemplatives.

That is why, very often, men of character and interior delicacy are repelled by the atmosphere of these monasteries, once they have spent a few months inside them, and leave in great discouragement, renouncing the interior life altogether.

However, if one finds himself in a cramped or rigid institution, he should not give in to anguish and despair. Nor should he waste time in futile acts of rebellion. Self-assertion is fatal to one's own interior *aspirations*.[28] If it is possible to find a wise director [*and follow him*],[29] then one should take account of the graces of God as much as possible, and not be afraid to follow them if the opportunity presents itself, even though this may mean going against the commonly accepted ideas. But at the same time one must avoid eccentricity, self-will, and vain show. If a person is really guided by the Holy Ghost, grace itself will take care of this, for exterior simplicity and obscurity are signs of grace. So too are meekness and obedience. Wherever there is a real conflict with obedience, he who gives in and obeys will never lose. He will always grow in grace and should not allow himself to feel frustrated by his sacrifice. But he who disobeys proudly will lose the grace of God.

Five Texts on Contemplative Prayer

Active contemplation presents no very special problem, but it would seem that passive or infused contemplation must, at least in its initial stages, be very difficult to recognize.[1] The elements of passivity, "unknowing" (or lack of clear conceptual knowledge of God as object) and the relative impotence or "ligature" of the spiritual faculties, would seem to reduce one to more or less complete helplessness in which he sees nothing, knows nothing, and is without any feeling or activity whatever. But surely mere emptiness is not enough. Is there any other sign? This problem, however, is in actual fact so abstract that it does not correspond to practical reality. Formulated in such terms, it may perhaps serve as a kind of algebraic equation to amuse scholars without intimate or direct knowledge of the contemplative experience. Otherwise, however, it is without meaning.

The truth is that contemplative intuition of the divine, known "not-as-object" and beyond concepts, is not purely negative at all. While our ordinary mode of knowing, feeling, and experiencing is indeed inhibited, there is a positive, though perhaps tenuous, awareness of God in an I-Thou relationship that, at least subjectively, does not admit of question.

This paradoxical "knowledge" without knowing is from one point of view very deficient: it lacks clarity and intellectual precision. It is almost impossible to reduce to logical formulation. But it is essentially beyond concepts and beyond logic. The simple conversational way of conveying this paradox is to say that without having any way of knowing how you know, you just know.

Does this knowledge admit of any doubt? Yes and no. On the conceptual level, where logic and rationality are in command, it may admit of doubt. In fact, it may perhaps admit of nothing else but doubt. It is so unrelated to reason as to seem perhaps irrational. But on another level it admits of no doubt. What is this other level? It is a level of immediate intuition in which an experience impresses itself upon us directly without ambiguity—a level on which we "experience" reality as we experience our own being. One does not have to prove that he exists: he knows it. He may doubt his ability to convince another of the fact. But one does not trouble to prove the obvious. Contemplative experience has about it an obviousness that is not arrived at through any step-by-step process. It is something you either "see" or don't see. It just bursts upon you, and is there.

This being the case, let us consider a few texts. They should be read carefully and meditatively.

1. St. John of the Cross

First, St. John of the Cross speaks of the emptiness and detachment with which one must respond to the secret inner inspiration to rest silently in the presence of God. The passivity of infused contemplation is emphasized:

> Endeavor then when the soul is reaching this state to detach it from all coveting of spiritual sweetness, pleasure and delight and meditation, and disturb it not with care or solicitude of any kind for higher things, still less for lower things, but bring it into the greatest possible degree of solitude and withdrawal. For the more the soul attains of all this and the sooner it reaches this restful tranquillity, the more abundantly does it become infused with the spirit of divine wisdom, which is the loving, tranquil, lonely, peaceful, sweet inebriator of the spirit. Hereby the soul feels itself to be gently and tenderly

wounded and ravished, *knowing not by whom, nor whence, nor how*. And the reason of this is that *the Spirit communicates Himself without any act on the part of the soul*. (*The Living Flame of Love*, iii, 38, vol. iii, 181)

2. Bl. John Ruysbroeck

Now a passage from Bl. John Ruysbroeck,[2] the great Flemish mystic of the fifteenth century [*sic*]. A difficult but sublime and full description of contemplative experience:

> This purity is the dwelling place of God within us, nor can any but God alone act upon it. It is eternal, and in it is neither time nor place, neither before nor after: but it is ever present, ready and manifest to such pure minds as may be raised up into it. In it we are all one, living in God and God in us. This simple unity is ever clear and manifest to the intellectual eyes when turned in upon the purity of the mind. It is a pure and serene air, lucent with divine light; and it is given to us to discover, fix and contemplate eternal truth with purified and illuminated eyes. Therein all things are of one form and become a single truth, a single image in the mirror of the wisdom of God: and when we look upon and practice it in the divine light with these same simple and spiritual eyes, then have we attained to the contemplative life. (*The Seven Steps of the Ladder of Spiritual Love*, VI, p. 56; London, 1944)

3. The Cloud of Unknowing

And now a beautifully simple explanation, contrasting with the above by its ingenuous clarity. It is from one of the best English treatises on contemplation: the fourteenth-century *Cloud of Unknowing*:[3]

> But now you put a question to me asking: "How shall I think about Him, and what is He?" And to this I can only answer you, "I do not know." With your question you have brought me into that same darkness and into that same cloud of unknowing into which I would wish you to be in yourself. Through grace a man can have great knowledge of all other creatures and

their works, and even of the works of God Himself, and he can think of them all; but of God Himself no man can think. *I would therefore leave all those things of which I can think and choose for my love that thing of which I cannot think.*

And why is this so? He may well be loved, but He may not be thought of. He may be reached and held close by means of love, but by means of thought, never. And therefore even though it is good occasionally to think of the kindness and the great worth of God in particular aspects, and even though it is a joy that is a proper part of contemplation, nevertheless in this work it should be cast down and covered with a cloud of forgetting.

You are to step above it with great courage and with determination and with a devout and pleasing stirring of love, and you are to try to pierce that darkness which is above you. You are to strike that thick cloud of unknowing with a sharp dart of longing love; and you are not to retreat no matter what comes to pass. (*The Cloud of Unknowing*, chap. VI; trans. Ira Progoff, New York, 1957, p. 72)

This admirable chapter of the *Cloud* contains all the solutions to the apparent problem raised a moment ago. How does one know that in the darkness of contemplation he "sees God"? He does not know. He sees God without knowing what he sees, because actually he sees nothing. His intellect is blinded by the "cloud," which hides the presence of the transcendent One. (This image of the Cloud hiding the Face of God goes back to Moses and Mount Sinai, and it has been interpreted in this particular sense since Philo Judaeus, Origen, and St. Gregory of Nyssa and by all the classical masters of Christian mysticism.) Even when there is no very definite experience of a hidden presence in the darkness of contemplation, there is always the positive and urgent movement of love which, on the one hand, wants to forget and "trample down" all clear knowledge of everything that is not God and, on the other, strives to "pierce the cloud of unknowing" with the "sharp dart" of its own longing. And the anonymous fourteenth-century writer gives his explanation, which is also that of St. Thomas Aquinas and St. John of the Cross. Though the essence of God cannot be adequately apprehended or clearly understood by man's intelligence, we can nevertheless *attain directly to Him by love,* and we do in fact realize obscurely in contemplation that by love we "reach Him and hold Him close." And when love reaches Him we are satisfied. Knowledge is of no importance. We know Him by love.

4. Meister Eckhart

Very much like Ruysbroeck is a Dominican contemporary of his in the Rhineland, Meister Eckhart. Eckhart has been out of favor with Catholic writers on mysticism due to the fact that twelve propositions taken from his works were condemned as heretical. But there is nothing heretical about the following passage, which is deep, subtle, and manifests a rich and vital mysticism, expressed in original language. Eckhart speaks of the mystical spark or center of the soul, the point of contact with God, not as something static and inert, but as a living and dynamic "agent." This "agent" makes God live in the soul and the soul in God, and consequently it is in everyone. But in many it has lost its life, through sin, and God is then "dead" to such souls. Yet the Father speaks to the soul in the words of Christ raising from the dead the son of the widow of Naim, and the agent comes back to life, recovering its capacity to "sense" the presence of God by love. This "agent" is the likeness of Christ in the soul; *it is our inmost self,*[4] the soul's spiritual life in God.

> Know then that God is present at all times in good people and that there is a Something in the soul in which God dwells. There is also a Something by which the soul lives in God, but when the soul is intent on external things that Something dies, and therefore God dies, as far as that soul is concerned. . . .
>
> The Father speaks through this noble agent (the Something) and says to His only-begotten Son: "Get up, young man!" Thus God—and the unity of God with the soul—is so complete as to seem incredible, since He is so high Himself as to be beyond the reach of intelligence. Nevertheless this agent reaches farther than heaven, yes, farther than the angels. . . . We want to reach far—far beyond measure—and yet we find that all that is to be understood or to be desired is still not God, *but that where mind and desire end, in that darkness, God shines.* (*Meister Eckhart: A Modern Translation,* Blakney, New York, 1957, p. 133)

5. St. Bernard of Clairvaux

We find much the same doctrine in St. Bernard of Clairvaux. The experience of God in darkness is definitely stated in this passage from a sermon on the Canticle:

> Take care not to imagine that in this union of the Word with the soul we believe there to be some bodily element. . . . This union is in the spirit, because God is a Spirit. . . . The Spouse receives Him by a special gift in her inmost heart, coming down from heaven, and all at once possesses Him whom she desires, not under any definite form, but obscurely infused; not appearing clearly but making His presence felt; and doubtless all the more delightful in that His presence is secret, and does not appear outwardly. This Word comes not sounding but penetrating; not speaking, but acting on the soul; not beating upon the ear but blandishing the heart. This is a Face that has no form, but impresses a form upon the soul; not striking the eyes of the body but making glad the countenance of the heart. (Sermon 31 *In Cantica*, n. 6)

It is impossible to render St. Bernard's Latin, in this passage, without taking great liberties and I have felt free to take them, in the hope that anyone who doubts the validity of my claims may go to the original and find how much more strongly and definitely St. Bernard himself speaks. This is one of those texts that requires deep meditation and study, and clearly it is filled with the same dynamic concept of the soul's union with God that we have glimpsed in Eckhart.

In all these texts, which could be multiplied for many more pages, we find the same elements. Rich metaphorical and symbolic language striving to indicate the reality, the directness of the intuition of God in contemplative prayer: an intuition that is deep, dynamic, living, beyond all comparison with the mere conceptual grasp of reality which man enjoys on his *ordinary*[5] level. Only one thing remains to be said, and it is clear to anyone who reads between the lines: that no amount of imagination and metaphor can begin to convey what is meant by contemplative experience of God present in one's own soul.

From this we can conclude that infused contemplation has a definitely positive element, dynamic, living, creative, transforming. It is a kind of interior revolution, drawing the soul inexplicably out of its normal routines of thought and desire to seek what cannot be thought and to grasp what lies beyond all desire.

The first sign of infused prayer is, then, this inexplicable and undaunted seeking, this quest that is not put off by aridity, or darkness, or frustration. On the contrary, in deepest darkness it finds peace, and in suffering it does not lack joy. Pure faith and blind hope are enough. Clear knowledge is not necessary.

The descriptions of the contemplative experience in these texts do not all view it on the same level. The passages quoted from *The Cloud of Unknowing* and from St. John of the Cross take it at its primary, most elementary stage. The other three, particularly that of Ruysbroeck, are more advanced. But we are concerned here most of all with the beginnings of contemplation. And it is clear that infused contemplation may begin before there is any definite experience of the presence of God. In other words, there is a kind of pre-experiential contemplation in which the soul simply plunges into the darkness without knowing why and tends blindly toward something it knows not. Only later is there a strong, subjective verification of the truth that this "something" toward which the soul is groping is really God Himself and not just an idea of God or a velleity for union with Him.

The mere fact of seeking Him blindly, undauntedly, in spite of dryness, in spite of the apparent hopelessness and irrationality of the quest, is, then, the first sign that this pre-experiential contemplation may be infused. Another sign would be the forgetfulness of ordinary cares and of the routine level of life in the darkness of prayer. Though the contemplative seeking for God may seem in a way quite senseless, yet in the depths of our soul it makes a great deal of sense, while, on the other hand, the seemingly rational preoccupations and projects of normal life now appear to be quite meaningless. This is important, because as a matter of fact a quite similar sense of meaninglessness is now prevalent everywhere and more or less affects every intelligent man. Not that everyone who feels the futility of life is ipso facto a contemplative. But the fact that *secular*[6] existence has begun to clearly manifest its own meaninglessness to everyone with eyes to see enables all sensitive and intelligent people to experience something akin to one of the phases of precontemplative purification. They can profit by this to learn a very healthy and fruitful spiritual detachment.

Finally,[7] a third sign that pre-experiential contemplation may have an infused character is the very definite and powerful sense of attraction which holds the soul prisoner in mystery. Although the soul is filled with a sense of affliction and defeat, *it has no desire to escape from this aridity.* Far from being attracted by legitimate pleasures and lights and relaxations of the natural order, it finds them repellent. All created goods only make it restless. They cannot satisfy it. Even spiritual consolations have lost their appeal and become tedious. But at the same time there is a growing conviction that joy and peace and fulfillment are only to be found somewhere in this lonely night of aridity and faith.

Sometimes this attraction is so powerful that it cancels out all the suffering felt by the soul, which counts its own pain and helplessness as nothing and becomes totally absorbed in this inexplicable desire for peace which it thinks can somehow be found in solitude and darkness. It follows the attraction, or rather allows itself to be drawn through the night of faith, by the power of an obscure love which it cannot yet understand.

Then suddenly comes the awakening to a new level of experience. The soul one day begins to realize, in a manner completely unexpected and surprising, that in this darkness it has found the living God. It is overwhelmed with the sense that He is there and that His love is surrounding and absorbing it on all sides. In fact, He has been there all the time—but He was utterly unknown. Now He is recognized. At that instant, there is no other important reality but God, infinite Love. Nothing else matters. The darkness remains as dark as ever and yet, somehow, it seems to have become brighter than *noonday.*[8] The soul has entered a new world, a world of rich experience that transcends the level of all other knowledge and all other love.

From then on its whole life is transformed. Although externally sufferings and difficulties and labors may be multiplied, the soul's interior life has become completely simple. It consists of one thought, one preoccupation, one love: GOD ALONE. In all things the eyes of the soul are upon Him. And this gaze of the soul includes in itself all adoration, all petition; it is continual sacrifice, it offers God unceasing reparation. It is perfect prayer, perfect worship. It is pure and simple love, that love which, as St. Bernard says, draws and absorbs every other activity of the soul into itself: *Amor caeteros in se omnes traducit et captivat affectus* (Sermon 83 *in Cantica*).[9] This love, infused into the soul by God, unifies all its powers and raises them up to Him, separating its desires and affections more and more from the world and from perishing things. Without realizing it, the soul makes rapid progress and becomes free, virtuous, and strong:[10] but it does not consider itself. It has no eyes for anything or anyone but God alone.

It has entered into the maturity of the spiritual life, the illuminative way, and is being drawn on toward complete union with God.[11]

[E I G H T]

The Paradox
of the Illuminative Way

The transition we have just described, the discovery of God as present to the inmost depths of our being, is in reality the shift from an exterior to an interior life in the strict sense of the word.[1] Broadly speaking, the term "interior life" is generally accepted as a valid description of any kind of striving after prayer and self-discipline, with a certain amount of reading, meditation, and emphasis on virtue. Strictly speaking, the interior life is a life in which this inner and spiritual consciousness has been awakened, and until the awakening has taken place, the "interior man" remains dead or at least dormant.

The life of the exterior man is a life of automatism, of unconsciously dictated thought and action, of mechanical conformity to the standards and prejudices of those around us—or, for that matter, of mechanical and compulsive revolt against them. For the rebellion against outward conformity is not what constitutes an interior life. On the contrary, it is usually only another form of compulsion, and indeed only another aspect of the *same* compulsion. It is a kind of negative conformity.

Now the people who live on this "automatic" level do not by any means realize to what an extent their lives are alienated and deprived of spontaneity. Their habits, their mechanical routines have acquired the power to satisfy them with a kind of pseudo-spontaneity, a kind of false naturalness. What is false and unspontaneous has become, to them, second nature. Hence what seems to them to be clear thinking is really confused thinking. What seems to them to be right willing is in fact craven evasion. What seems to them to be freedom is mere compulsion. Not of course that they are not morally responsible for their acts. No, they are sane and "free," and yet to a surprising extent they lack sanity and freedom, if their lives are looked at from the point of view of the interior and spiritual man. And this is true of us all: for even the spiritual are not always spiritual. Perhaps they have only rare moments of "awakening" when they see their ordinary life as it really is—and then they fall back into captivity.

The paradox of the illuminative way is, then, that the awakening and enlightening of the inner man goes with the darkening and the blinding of the exterior man. As our inner spiritual consciousness awakens, our exterior and worldly consciousness is befuddled and hampered in its action. This is a preliminary stage, one of transition, for when our minds have been perfectly spiritualized, then there is no failure on the part of the exterior consciousness, which has now become subordinated to and indeed an aspect of inner and contemplative awareness.

But the point that most needs to be emphasized is that when the inner consciousness begins to be awakened, it is necessary to darken and put to sleep even the discursive and rational lights with which we were familiar in meditation. Here it must be said that the individual himself does not have to make a special effort to do this work of darkening. It is begun and carried on for him by the action of God, and therefore it is largely passive. However, cooperation is necessary until such time as the passivity becomes so strong that the soul cannot place any obstacles in the way of the infused light, which is darkness. And cooperation will consist in *not struggling* to carry on the familiar laborious habits of prayer and devotion, which have hitherto proved satisfying and useful. As soon as it appears that this labor is no longer of value—that is to say, when it definitely seems to obstruct the more peaceful, mysterious, and attractive force of passive absorption—then the labor should be abandoned.

The problem here is that habit is strong and automatism speaks with the authority of a pseudo-conscience. One feels guilty in relaxing and resting in darkness. There is no rational basis for this guilt, once we realize that our "reaching" into the darkness really implies a serious and energetic effort of faith, and that our persisting in arid prayer requires a great deal of courage and patience. But no, we feel that we ought to be following the "safe" routine that has the advantage of being "normal" and "accepted," rather than advancing into this unknown darkness where we are without support from any other human consciousness, without contact with others, and forced to walk on our own unsteady feet. Not only that, but we feel very much as if we had started walking on water. The impulse to climb back into the boat of secure habit and convention is almost uncontrollable.

This is not a matter of mere fancy. The urgency of the problem comes from the fact that when we begin to be frequently absorbed in the passivity of pre-experiential contemplation (and this goes also for masked contemplation, which is just about the same thing), we feel that we are losing our ability to meditate and pray. Not only that, but we believe, and even have evidence for the fact, that we are not as virtuous as we had thought. (This realization is of course one of the most valuable and enviable effects of infused prayer!) We begin to see the nonentity and triviality of our exterior self: and since we are still completely identified with that exterior self, this means that to all intents and purposes we begin to experience ourselves as evil, ungodly, hypocritical, and utterly contemptible beings. We *should* experience this. For as long as we live in our exterior consciousness alone and identify ourselves completely with the superficial and transient side of our existence, then we are completely immersed in unreality. And to cling with passion to a state of unreality is the root of all sin, technically known as pride. It is the affirmation of our nonbeing as the ultimate reality for which we live, as against the being and truth of God. Hence we must become detached from the unreality that is in us in order to be united to the reality that lies deeper within and is our true self—our *inmost*[2] self-in-God.

Insofar as our spiritual life consists of thoughts, desires, actions, devotions, and projects of our exterior self, it participates in the nonbeing and the falsity of that exterior self. Of course, there is no such thing as a purely exterior spirituality. No matter how external our spiritual life may be, if it has a root of sincerity, it is based in the interior man and therefore has value and reality in the sight of God. But the purpose of our life is to bring *all* our strivings and desires into the sanctuary of the inner self and place them all under the command of an inner and God-inspired consciousness. This is the work of grace.

The great paradox of the illuminative way, when the mystical life begins and when progress becomes serious, is that it gives the bewildering impression that all spiritual life has collapsed and that progress is at an end. One suddenly seems to be going backwards. And the reason for this is that the spiritual life is now no longer the result of our own, stumbling, limited, conscious efforts, but is produced by the hidden action of God within us, and almost always *in spite of* us. When passive contemplation begins, there is a definite sense of struggle and opposition: it is the battle of Jacob with the angel, of the inner man with the exterior man, and the battle of the fallen soul with God, one of the subjects of the great hermetic drama of Blake's Prophetic books. Here is the text from Genesis that is the prototype of all such spiritual battles:

> Jacob remained alone and, behold, a man wrestled with him until morning. And when he saw that he could not overcome him, he touched the sinew of his thigh and forthwith it shrank. And he said to him, Let me go, for it is the break of day. He answered, I will not let thee go except thou bless me. And he said: What is thy name? And he answered: Jacob. But he said: Thy name shall not be called Jacob but Israel, for if thou hast been strong against God, how much more shalt thou prevail against men? Jacob asked him: By what name art thou called? He answered, Why dost thou ask me my name? And he blessed him in the same place. (Genesis 32:24–29)

The battle is with "man" and yet it is with God, for it is the battle of our exterior self with the interior self, the "agent" which is the likeness of God in our soul and which appears at first sight to be utterly opposed to the only self we know. It is the battle of our own strength, lodged in the exterior self, with the strength of God, which is the life and actuality of our interior self. And in the battle, which takes place in the darkness of night, the angel, the inner self, wounds a nerve in our thigh so that afterwards we limp. Our natural powers are restricted and crippled. We are humbled and made ignorant. We see that we have become foolish and that even in good works we limp and are feeble. But also, though we are drawn to evil, we no longer have the power to run swiftly in pursuit of it. Yet we have power over our antagonist to the extent that, though we cannot overcome him, yet we do not let him go until he blesses us. This power is more than our own strength; it is the power of love, and it secretly comes from within, from the antagonist Himself. It is His own power with which He wishes to be held by us. It is the power by which He is "reached and held close" according to *The Cloud of Unknowing*. It makes us "strong against God" and merits for us a new name, Israel, which means "He who sees God." And this new name is what makes us contemplatives—it is a new being and a new capacity for experience. Yet when we ask the name of our antagonist, we cannot know it, for even our own inmost self is unknown, just as God Himself is unknown.

St. John of the Cross explains in considerable detail the purification of the soul by the infused light of God. There are, to be exact, two levels of purification. There is purification of the exterior and interior senses, which is a kind of preliminary to the full mystical life. This is called the "dark night of sense" and is the ordinary threshold over which we pass into mystical contemplation. Then there is a deeper and more terrible night, the "dark night of the spirit," in which we pass on to perfect union with God.

In the dark night of sense, the exterior self is purified and to a great extent, though not completely, destroyed. But in the dark night of the spirit even the interior man is purified. These two nights are two spiritual deaths. In the first, the exterior man "dies" to rise and become the inner man. In the second the interior man dies and rises so completely united to God that the two are one and there remains no division between them except the metaphysical distinction of natures. It is, then, as if the soul itself were God and God were the soul or, even more, as if the soul were completely lost in God "as a drop of water in a flagon of purest wine."

In any case, the routine, confused, compulsive, and self-seeking activity of the soul must be completely transformed into the spiritual, free, illuminated, and God-centered activity of perfect love. Everything in the soul that is repugnant to God's will and God's love must be completely destroyed.

> Since no creature whatsoever or any of its actions and abilities can conform or can attain to that which is God, therefore must the soul be stripped of all things created and of its own actions and abilities—namely of its understanding, liking and feeling—so that when all that is unlike God and unconformed to Him is cast out, the soul may receive the likeness of God; and nothing will then remain in it that is not the will of God and it will thus be transformed in God. (*Ascent of Mount Carmel,* ii, v, 4; vol. I, p. 80)

In the present book we are concerned almost entirely with the beginnings of infused contemplation and therefore we can concentrate on the night of the senses, which brings us into the illuminative way of contemplation. And the first thing to do is to realize and appreciate the fact that, for all the suffering and bewilderment of this night and all its apparent frustrations, it is a very great gift of God, a grace to which we should try to correspond with all the power and all the love of our hearts.

What to Do: The Teaching of St. John of the Cross

St. John of the Cross[1] explains in great detail how the soul should behave in order to accept this great gift of God and make use of it without spoiling His work.[2] It is very important to have competent guidance and instruction in the ways of contemplative prayer. Otherwise it will be almost impossible to avoid errors and obstacles. The reason for this is that no matter how good the intentions of the soul may be, its natural coarseness and clumsiness still prevent it from sensing the full import of the delicate work performed by God's love within its most intimate depths and cooperating with His action.

The most important thing of all is to get some realization of what God is doing in your soul. Learn the tremendous value of this obscure and sometimes crucifying light of faith, which darkens and empties your mind with respect to all natural convictions and leads you into realms without evidence in order to bring you to the threshold of an actual experimental contact with the living God. In fact, St. John of the Cross does not hesitate to say that this darkness is caused by the presence of God in the intellect,

blinding our finite powers by the brightness of His unlimited
actuality and truth.

> This Dark Night *is the inflowing of God into the soul which*
> *purges it* of its ignorances and imperfections, natural and spiri-
> tual, and which is called by contemplatives infused contempla-
> tion. . . . *Herein God secretly teaches the soul and instructs it in*
> *perfection of love without its doing anything or understanding*
> *of what manner is this infused contemplation.* (*Dark Night,* II, v, 1)

And so you will see that, in order to cooperate with this great
work of grace in your soul, you must not desire or seek the things
which God's immense light is striving to drive out of you, that He
may replace them by His own truth. Do not therefore lament when
your prayer is empty of all precise, rational knowledge of God and
when you cannot seize Him any longer by clear, definite concepts.
Do not be surprised or alarmed when your will no longer finds
sweetness or consolation in the things of God and when your imagination is darkened and thrown into disorder. You are out of your
depth; your mind and will have been led beyond the borders of
nature and they can no longer function as they used to because
they are in the presence of a reality[3] that overwhelms them. This
is precisely as God wants it to be, for He Himself is that reality[4]
and He is now beginning to infuse into the soul His own Light and
His own Love in one general confused experience of mute attraction and peaceful desire. Do not seek anything more precise than
this for the moment. If you attempt by your action to increase the
precision of your knowledge of God or to intensify the feeling of
love, you will interfere with His work and He will withdraw His
light and His grace, leaving you with the fruit of your own mis-
guided natural activity.

The natural appetite of your mind and will for their own particular kind of satisfaction will suffer and rebel against this
seemingly hard regime: but remember that, as the saint says: "*By*
means of this dark and loving knowledge God is united to the soul

in a lofty and divine degree. For this dark and loving knowledge which is faith serves as a means to divine union in this life even as in the next life the light of glory serves as an intermediary to the clear vision of God" (*Ascent of Mount Carmel,* ii, 24).

Do not, then, stir yourself up to useless interior activities. Avoid everything that will bring unnecessary complications into your life. Live in as much peace and quiet and retirement as you can, and do not go out of your way to get involved in labors and duties, no matter how much glory they may seem to give to God. Do the tasks appointed to you as perfectly as you can with disinterested love and great peace in order to show your desire of pleasing God. Love and serve Him peacefully and in all your works preserve recollection. Do what you do quietly and without fuss. Seek solitude as much as you can; dwell in the silence of your own soul and rest there in the simple and simplifying light which God is infusing into you. Do not make the mistake of aspiring to the spectacular "experiences" that you read about in the lives of great mystics. None of those graces (called *gratis datae*) can sanctify you nearly so well as this obscure and purifying light and love of God which is given you to no other end than to make you perfect in His love.

Passing beyond all that can be known and understood both spiritually and naturally, *the soul will desire with all desire to come to that* WHICH CANNOT BE KNOWN, NEITHER CAN ENTER INTO ITS HEART. And leaving behind *all that it experiences and feels both temporally and spiritually* and all that it is able to experience in this life, IT WILL DESIRE WITH ALL DESIRE TO COME TO THAT WHICH SURPASSES FEELING AND EXPERIENCE. (*Ascent of Mount Carmel,* ii, 3)

Do not be too anxious about your advancement in the ways of prayer, because you have left the beaten track and are traveling by paths that cannot be charted and measured. Therefore leave God to take care of your degree of sanctity and of contemplation.

If you yourself try to measure your own progress, you will waste your time in futile introspection. Seek one thing alone: to purify your love of God more and more, to abandon yourself more and more perfectly to His will and to love Him more exclusively and more completely, but also more simply and more peacefully and with more total and uncompromising trust.[5]

Here is a letter written by St. John of the Cross to one of his penitents who was afflicted with anxiety and fear in the darkness of her contemplation, wondering if she were deluded, and tempted to turn back:

> While you are walking in this darkness and in these empty places of spiritual poverty you think that everything and everyone are failing you; but that is not surprising, for at these times it seems to you that God too is failing you. But nothing is failing you, nor have you any need to consult me about anything, nor have you any reason to do so, nor do you know one, nor will you find one: this is merely suspicion without cause. He that seeks naught but God walks not in darkness, in whatever darkness and poverty he may find himself; and he that harbors no presumptuousness and desires not his own satisfaction either as to God or as to the creatures, and works his own will in naught soever, has no need to stumble or to worry about anything. You are progressing well: remain in quietness and rejoice. . . .
>
> Never have you been in a better state than now, for never have you been humbler or more submissive nor have you ever counted yourself and everything in the world as of such little worth . . . nor have you ever served God so purely and disinterestedly as now, nor do you any longer go, as perchance you were wont, after the imperfections of your will and your own interest. (Letter xviii, to Doña Juana de Pedraza)

Here we have all the things one needs to remember in traveling by the dark path of contemplation: to leave everything in the hands of God; to cease from all worries and anxieties; to believe and trust in Him, and look at Him alone, not turning aside to examine your own pleasures and pains, or to seek your own satisfaction in anything. Above all you give up your own will and your own whims and act not according to your own desires, but according to the objective will of God and the promptings of that grace which leads us always in the ways of emptiness and peace.

For the graces and inspirations of the Holy Spirit do not come to the contemplative soul in the form of strong and ardent desires for some personal satisfaction or achievement. When such things arise in us and oppose themselves to obedience, we must always suspect them. The grace of contemplation leads always in the path of humility, obscurity, and emptiness.

> That man will not be able to attain to perfection who endeavours not to be satisfied with nothing, so that his natural and spiritual concupiscence may be content with emptiness; for this is needful if a man would attain to the highest tranquility and peace of spirit; and in this way the love of God is almost continually in action in the simple and pure soul. (*Maxims,* 51)

If you are sincere in following this path, you will be glad to welcome the trials [*and crosses*][6] God sends you, and although they may cause intense and baffling pain to your soul, you will take them in all peace and meekness and interior joy, realizing the love that comes with them from God and resting in the assurance that He is using these instruments to renew His likeness in your soul.

Sanctity and contemplation are only to be found in the purity of love. The true contemplative is not one who has the most exalted visions of the Divine Essence, but one who is most closely united to God in faith and love and allows himself to be absorbed and transformed into Him by the Holy Ghost. To such a soul everything becomes a source and occasion of love.

> Even as the bee extracts from all plants the honey that is in them and has no use for them for aught else save for that purpose, *even so the soul with great facility extracts the sweetness of love that is in all things that pass through it. IT LOVES GOD IN EACH OF THEM, WHETHER PLEASANT OR UNPLEASANT. (Spiritual Canticle,* xxvii)

To such a soul the pleasant or unpleasant accidents of things and events gradually fade away and disappear from sight. The only thing that matters is to please the Beloved, and since in all things we can please Him by appreciating the love He sends to us in them, the contemplative finds equal joy in the pleasures and pains of mortal existence, in the sorrows as well as the delights of daily life. "For the soul knows naught but love, and its pleasure in all things and occupations is ever the delight of the love of God" (*Spiritual Canticle*, xxvii).

St. John of the Cross uses strong words to tell us of the value of contemplation:

Let those that are great actives and think to girdle the world with their outward works take note that *they would bring far more profit to the Church and be far more pleasing to God if they spent even half this time in abiding with God in prayer.* . . . Of a surety they would accomplish more with one piece of work than they now do with a thousand and that with far less labour. (*Spiritual Canticle*, xxix, 3)

And he adds:

A very little of this pure (mystical) love is precious in the sight of God and of greater profit to the Church than are all works together. (*Spiritual Canticle*, xxix, 3)[7]

TEN

Some Dangers

The words of St. John of the Cross must be understood in the context of the saint's own life.[1] He was not preaching an absolute
repudiation of all duties and responsibilities and all works and
labors for the Church of God or for other men. He and St. Teresa
of Avila, the greatest contemplatives of their time, were also
very active and labored and suffered much for the reform of the
Carmelite Order. But the meaning of St. John's argument is this:
activities prompted by our own tastes and ambitions will be rid-
dled with imperfection and will always tend to disturb the union
of our soul with God. On the other hand, God desires to bring us to
this perfect union with Him *in order that our minds and wills, perfectly united and absorbed by Him, may act in perfect harmony and
coordination with Him, as free instruments of His love and mercy.*
Thus He uses contemplatives to communicate His love to other men.

The heresy of quietism, on the other hand, encloses a man
within himself in an entirely selfish solitude which excludes not
only other men but even God Himself. Quietism, while bearing a
superficial resemblance to Christian contemplation, is actually
its complete contradiction. The contemplative empties himself of
every created love in order to be filled with the love of God
alone, and divests his mind of all created images and phantasms in

order to receive the pure and simple light of God directly into the summit of his soul. The quietist, on the other hand, pursuing a false ideal of absolute "annihilation" of his own soul, seeks to empty himself of *all* love and *all* knowledge and remain inert in a kind of spiritual vacuum in which there is no motion, no thought, no apprehension, no act of love, no passive receptivity, but a mere blank without light or warmth or breath of interior life. Thus the quietist imagines that he is being passively moved by God.

Christian contemplation, being produced in the soul by the most sublime and delicate action of infused love, makes the soul perfect in the love of God while perfecting all other virtues in that same contemplative love. But to the quietist the quest for virtue is "self-love" and the desire of heaven is also "self-love." The hope of union with God in heaven is considered mercenary. The desire to practice virtue and avoid sin is regarded as an "imperfection," because it supposedly troubles the "peace" of the "annihilated" soul.

Christian contemplation is the perfection of love, and quietism is the exclusion of all love. Actually it is the quintessence of selfishness, because the quietist encloses himself in his own shell and keeps himself in a torpor in order to shut out all the painful realities of life which Christ would have us *face with faith and abandonment.*[2] The "prayer" of the quietist is no prayer at all, because the mind and will are entirely inert and dead: that is to say, they remain completely inactive while a constant stream of distractions and temptations is allowed to pour through them passively without the slightest show of effort to counteract them by conscious attention to God or to anything else.

If your contemplation is a complete blank or a mere spiritual chaos, without any love or desire of God, then be persuaded that you are not a contemplative. But, on the other hand, remember that in the beginning of contemplation as well as in times of great trial, the desire and awareness of God are something so deep, so mute, and so tenuous that it is hard to realize their presence at all. However, a glance is sufficient to tell you that they are there. In fact, the true contemplative suffers from the fact that he thinks he is without desire of God, and that very suffering bears witness to his desire. This suffering itself is often the work of infused love. Therefore the Christian contemplative, even when he fears that his prayer is hopelessly sterile and distracted, contradicts his own fears by the very intensity of *the anguish with which he longs for God*. If you feel that anguish and longing, be satisfied that you are not a quietist. Continue to seek God in love and self-abasement, and you will find Him.

Do not think, therefore, that in order to avoid quietism you must force yourself to meditate and produce acts and affections when this has become practically impossible. On the contrary, that would be fatal to God's work in your soul, if the signs of contemplation described above are verified in you.

Be content to remain in loneliness and isolation, dryness and anguish, waiting upon God in darkness. Your inarticulate longing for Him in the night of suffering will be your most eloquent prayer. It will be more valuable to you and to the Church and will give more glory to God than the highest natural flights of the intelligence or the imagination. But be persuaded, on the contrary, that God is here working to raise your intellect and will to the highest perfection of supernatural activity in union with His Holy Spirit. By pouring His Wisdom into your soul, he is accomplishing the greatest work of His love, forming the perfect likeness of Christ, His incarnate Word, in you, and perfecting His Church through everything that you allow Him to perform by the agency of your free will transformed and elevated in Him. Praise and glorify God, you who have tasted the first fruits of this marvelous grace, and pray to Him to continue His great work in your soul. Withdraw yourself from all care; trust not in yourself but in Him; do not be anxious or solicitous to perform great works for Him until He leads you Himself, by obedience and love and the events which His Providence directs, to undertake the works He has planned for you and by which He will use you to communicate the fire of His love to other men.[3]

Because of the superficial resemblance between contemplation and quietism, especially on paper, it has become customary and even perhaps necessary for one who writes on Christian mysticism to make sure that the reader does not confuse these two things. The danger is not so much that there might be a lot of people who systematically follow quietism to its logical conclusion, but that a few, not realizing the difference between negative inactivity and positive contemplation, might simply become disoriented at the very start and renounce certain necessary efforts and concerns. There can always be a tendency for contemplatives to accept the inevitable emptiness of their life too philosophically and make a virtue out of defeat. In this, the modern contemplative finds himself traveling in much the same territory as the existentialist. Indeed, it is possible that the one aspect of religion which might still remain attractive to a *nonreligious*[4] existentialist would be this lonely, desolate darkness of prayer in which the solitary believer commits himself to a heroic risk, and stakes everything he has and is on his decision to walk in the darkness beyond concepts, hoping that he can find that ultimate Reality which concepts are inadequate to describe.

But here again the difference is much greater than it seems to be. There is an infinite distance between the acceptance of one's own absolute autonomy, one's "absurd" freedom, as the only reality in an "absurd" universe and the acceptance of the transcendent and Divine Reality behind the apparent absurdity of everyday life. Here again, it is the difference between a man who is shut up in himself and cannot open his heart to any other being and the man who has forgotten himself and become lost in Being.

One thing the existentialist and the contemplative have in common is their refusal to base their lives entirely on the passive acceptance of words which purport to describe essences with which no one is really concerned. The Protestant theologian Paul Tillich[5] has been treated as a radical because he defined faith as an "ultimate concern." But in this frankly existentialist definition he was doubtless reacting against the complacent way in which pious folk have more and more come to use the formulas and concepts of revealed religion in order to *avoid* concern. Ours is an age of decadent (and I hope renascent) religion. Our contemporaries, especially those who have gone in for popular religion, have often reduced faith to a comfortable assent to slogans without meaning. In assuming the reality of essences and beings that could not be verified by scientific experiment, too many have merely freed themselves from any sense of responsibility to a vague God Who, they were told, existed and took care of these important matters Himself. The ordinary person should occupy himself frankly and completely with a secular existence, moneymaking, pleasure, and success. His prudent excursions into the realm of the sacred should be limited to a few prayers and communal gestures that were necessary to bring God to his aid in achieving secular purposes. Such "faith" is of course merely a modern superstition, and Tillich's definition was probably framed to exclude it entirely from serious consideration.

Both the existentialist and the contemplative are united by the depth and sincerity of their "concern." Both reject any easy or convenient substitute for ultimate reality. Both face the insecurity and darkness of spiritual risk. And here, of course, we face the need to distinguish between the religious and irreligious existentialist. The fact is that, though Sartre,[6] popularly regarded as "the" existentialist, is also an atheist, more existentialist thinkers are religious than otherwise. Kierkegaard, who is regarded as the father of them all, was one of the great religious geniuses of an irreligious century. Men like Gabriel Marcel (a Catholic)[7] and Nicholas Berdyaev (a Russian Orthodox)[8] have entered fully into his heritage. Jacques Maritain,[9] who has written a very understanding Thomist critique of existentialism, is also a Christian contemplative whose contemplation has attuned him to the subjective sorrow and sincerity of existentialism while protecting him from its nihilistic dangers.

It is clear that if a dialogue is to take place between Christians and the subjectivists of our time, a contemplative is the one to speak for Christianity. A dogmatist, firmly entrenched in scholastic categories, has no way of making himself understood. If he is to enter a fruitful dialogue with some opposite number, he had better look to the camp of the Marxists. There too he will find dogma, authority, and "true believers." Whether or not he will be able to make contact with them is another matter, but in any case it should be clear that the contemplative and the Marxist have no common ground. They do not think in the same way or even see the same things at all. To be a Marxist one would have to repress all the inner, personal "concern" with spiritual fulfillment and lose oneself in the collective mystery of the revolution. Contemplation could only interest a Marxist if it caught him on the rebound after a fall from dialectical grace and at a moment when his interior starvation demanded, by accident, to be recognized. But a writer like Boris Pasternak,[10] himself never a Marxist, bears witness to the intense hunger for a spiritual experience of reality which has remained alive in the arid desert of Russian materialism since 1917. Not that Pasternak is a contemplative in the full sense of the word, but his poetry and poetic prose are filled with symbolic intuitions on the order of *theoria physike,* and his view of life is in a broad sense not only Christian, but mystical. This of course marks him out as a complete heretic in Russia, where "mysticism" is the ultimate term of contempt.

However, there is in Marxism enough of false mysticism and religiosity to seduce anyone who hungers after some substitute for spiritual religion. There is no question that the demand for "faith" and for self-sacrifice which is made by Marxism is a much more solid and human reality than the irresponsible pseudo-Christianity that still flourishes in certain societies devoted entirely to secular values. There is some *spiritual*[11] danger in Marxism and in the pseudo-contemplation which its worldview implies. This danger lies in a crypto-religious appeal it offers to those who have no stomach left for the empty forms of popular religion in which the concept "god" has died of exhaustion.

To return to more urgent problems of the contemplative life: the one great danger that confronts every man who takes spiritual experience seriously is the danger of illuminism or, in Mgr. Knox's term, "enthusiasm."[12] Here the problem is that of taking one's subjective experience so seriously that it becomes more important than truth, more important than God. Once spiritual experience becomes objectified, it turns into an idol. It becomes a "thing," a "reality" which we serve. We were not created for the service of any "thing," but for the service of God alone, Who is not and cannot be a "thing." To serve Him Who is no "object" is freedom. To live for spiritual experience is slavery, and such slavery makes the contemplative life just as secular (though in a more subtle way) as the service of any other "thing," no matter how base: money, pleasure, success. Indeed, the ruin of many potential contemplatives has been this avidity for spiritual success. This is why at the very beginning of this essay I stressed the danger of looking for "happiness" as a goal in the life of contemplation. It is all the more dangerous because the satisfaction we derive from spiritual things is pure and perfect. And all the harder to bring under objective criticism.

Hence the danger of attaching an exclusive importance to what we ourselves experience and of believing that every intuition comes to us from God. The worst errors can be taken for truth when a man has forgotten how to criticize the movements that arise in his heart dressed in the light of inspiration.

In recent years there have been some much publicized experiments with the use of drugs to induce spiritual experience. For a long time it had been known that peyote helped to induce a kind of ecstasy in the rites of an Indian tribe. Researchers and clinicians had also begun to experiment with mescaline and lysergic acid in the treatment of alcoholism and mental trouble. It was found that these drugs frequently produced profound experiences resembling those of the mystics. In some cases there were visions and ecstasies, in others negative experiences of horror and despair. But the action of the drug seemed to help open up undiscovered and unknown depths in the ones who took them. Aldous Huxley[13] has gone into this question with the set purpose of finding out whether these experiences were, or were not, truly spiritual. It is his opinion that they are. He bases his judgment on his own experiments with mescaline and lysergic acid and on the reports of others who have used them experimentally or under treatment.

Whatever may be the final outcome of these experiments, they are to be viewed with extreme caution. Assuming that the facts are correct, and there is no reason to doubt the reported experiences, there is still no reason to conclude that because such things are possible, therefore they ought to be done. On the contrary, it seems to me that we would run the risk of organized and large-scale illuminism. This would mean that an easily available spiritual experience would be sought for its own sake. But this kind of attachment is just as dangerous, if not more dangerous, than any other. St. John of the Cross, for example, has warned against too readily consenting even to visions and inspirations that have every appearance of coming gratuitously and direct from God.

Although all these things may happen to the bodily senses in the way of God we must never rely on them or admit them, but we must always fly from them, without trying to ascertain whether they be good or evil; for the more completely exterior and corporeal they are, the less certainly are they of God. . . . So he that esteems such things errs greatly and places himself in great peril of deception; and at best he will have in himself a complete impediment to the attainment of spirituality. (*Ascent of Mount Carmel,* ii, xi, 2–3)

This is a very important observation, because it shows that what really matters in spiritual experience is not its interiority, or its natural purity, or the joy, light, exaltation, and transforming effect it may seem to have: these things are secondary and accidental. What matters is not what one feels, but *what really takes place* beyond the level of feeling or experience. In genuine contemplation, what takes place is a contact between the inmost reality of the created person and the infinite Reality of God. The *experience* which accompanies this contact may be a more or less faithful sign of what has taken place. But the experience, the vision, the intuition, is only a sign and is, furthermore, capable of being dissociated from any reality and being a mere empty figure. The illuminist is one who attaches himself to the sign, the experience, without regard for the invisible substance of a contact which transcends experience.

This is not to say that an experience produced by the use of a drug *cannot* be associated with anything supernatural. God is master of His gifts and can give them in any way He likes. But the point is that the danger of deception is here very great. So that I would be inclined to say, as a personal opinion, that the gravest peril that faces the contemplative today is this specious temptation to illuminism. I can only regard with the greatest uneasiness the *falsification*[14] and corruption of *mystical*[15] religion that might arise from the abuse of these dangerous methods. No one who wants to be a contemplative should take such drugs for purely spiritual reasons. He should only consent to their use if they are prescribed as *medically*[16] necessary by a qualified physician. As far as I know, doctors will not be too quick to give such prescriptions.

The true contemplative is a lover of sobriety and obscurity. He prefers all that is quiet, humble, unassuming. He has no taste for spiritual excitements. They easily weary him. His inclination is to that which seems to be nothing, which tells him little or nothing, which promises him nothing. Only one who can remain at peace in emptiness, without projects or vanities, without speeches to justify his own apparent uselessness, can be safe from the fatal appeal of those spiritual impulses that move him to assert himself and "be something" in the eyes of other men. But the contemplative is, of all religious men, the one most likely to realize that he is not a saint and least anxious to appear one in the eyes of others. He is, in fact, delivered from subjection to appearances and cares very little about them. At the same time, since he has neither the inclination nor the need to be a rebel, he does not have to advertise his contempt for appearances. He simply neglects them. They no longer interest him. He is quite content to be considered an idiot, if necessary, and in this he has a long tradition behind him. Long ago St. Paul said he was glad to be a "fool for the sake of Christ." The oriental Church has its holy madmen, the *yurodivi*, imitated on occasion in the West by men like St. Francis of Assisi and many others. The contemplative does not need to be systematic about anything, even about apparent madness. He is content with the wisdom of God, which is folly to men not because it is contrary to the wisdom of man, but because it entirely transcends it.

ELEVEN

Contemplation
and Neurosis

Since we are speaking of madness, let us for a moment seriously consider the question whether contemplation puts so much strain on the mind that most normal men are not able to bear it. To break down under strain is not "folly for the sake of Christ," except if it happens to someone through no fault of his own, in pursuit of a genuine duty. But certainly there is nothing holy about a presumptuous spiritual ambition that would drive a man to mental breakdown in pursuit of a spiritual illusion—or even in quest of genuine contemplation.

First of all, it is true that the contemplative life requires special mental and spiritual aptitudes, and one who does not have the necessary gifts should not presume to push his way into affairs that are beyond his capacity. I do not mean necessarily that contemplatives form a special elite. Nor am I speaking only of the contemplative life in its canonical sense: life in a cloistered religious order. No one can give himself completely and seriously to contemplation as I have described it, unless he is mentally and spiritually prepared. The contemplative life is one of intense inner conflict. The peace which it brings is a peace that follows war, and exists often enough in the midst of war. Anyone who is already divided against himself, and at war with himself, had better get himself together before he *sets out to conquer this realm*[1] of ascetic meditation and contemplative prayer. Otherwise the divisions already present in him will tear him apart in short order.

Excursions into the recollected darkness of contemplation are tempting to anyone with a schizoid character, because it is easy to mistake schizoid withdrawal for contemplative recollection. And a few formulas of contemplative jargon may offer themselves as fatally convenient opportunities for rationalization by one who is merely escaping, within himself, from external reality.

Contemplation does not back away from reality or evade it. It sees through superficial being and goes beyond it. This implies a full acceptance of things as they are and a sane evaluation of them. The "darkness" of the contemplative night is not a rejection of created things. On the contrary, the contemplative in some way "finds" and discovers things as they really are, and enjoys them in a higher way when he rises above contacts with them that are merely sensual and superficial. As St. John of the Cross says:

> Through the eye that is purged of the joy of sight, there comes a spiritual joy directed to God in all things that are seen, whether divine or profane. Through the ear that is purged from the joy of hearing there comes to the soul a joy most spiritual and a hundredfold directed to God in all that it hears, whether it be divine or profane. Even so is it with the other senses when they are purged. For even as in the state of innocence all that our first parents saw and said and ate in Paradise furnished them with [the] greater sweetness of contemplation . . . even so the man whose sense is purged from all things of sense and made subject to the spirit, receives in the very first motion the delight of delectable knowledge and contemplation of God. (*Ascent of Mount Carmel,* ii, xxvi, 5)

The neurotic, on the other hand, cannot accept reality as it is. He withdraws into himself and, if he sees things at all, sees only that aspect of them which he can bear to see, and no other. Or at least he tries to.

Now it is easy to understand that an unwise and Manichean type of asceticism can give a person a pathological attitude toward reality. In such case there is great danger of his becoming a pseudo-mystic who flees into his own inner darkness and tries to wall himself up inside his own silence. There he seeks to enjoy the false sweetness of a narcissistic seclusion, and does indeed enjoy it for a while until he learns, too late, that he has poisoned himself with the fruit of a tree that is forbidden.

Here again, we notice a deep symbolic wisdom in Patristic interpretations of the story of the Fall in Genesis. This indeed is the forbidden tree: this tree of self, which grows in the middle of Paradise, but which we ourselves are not supposed to see or notice. All the other trees are there, and they refresh us with their fruits. Of them we can be aware, and they are there to be enjoyed for the love of God. But if we become aware of ourselves, turn back too much upon ourselves, and seek to rest in ourselves, then we take the fruit that was forbidden us: we become "as gods, knowing good and evil," for we find division within ourselves and are cut off from external reality at the same time. The "nothingness" within us—which is at the same time the place where our freedom springs into being—is secretly filled with the presence and light of God as long as our eyes are not on ourselves. And then our freedom is united with the freedom of God Himself. Nothing can impede the joy and creativity of our acts of love. But when we look at the source of freedom within us, become too conscious of it, examine it, and subject it to planned and conscious mastery, then the presence and power of God withdraw (for God does not want to be seen at work), and we remain confronted with our own nothingness. At that precise moment, we lose our freedom and become the captives of anxiety.

This is nowhere more true than in the life of contemplation, and the neurotic cannot help but self-consciously exploit his opportunities for spiritual "experience." He is compelled to do this to allay his anxiety and to justify his withdrawal from reality as a religious act. In actual fact his contemplation is a lie, an act of idolatry, and forms part of his private religion. For such men as this, the solitude and freedom of the contemplative life lead only to ruin. They are not capable of solitude because they are not strong enough in love.

The pseudo-contemplative darkness of the schizoid is a trancelike and strained imposture. In this false recollection, the only escape from the iron grip of self-consciousness is a fall into a dazed, dreamlike torpor. In genuine contemplation one normally begins with quiet and detached intuitions, simple peace, interior silence. There is little or no preoccupation with self. If one finds himself reflecting too much on himself, he instinctively breaks the false absorption by turning to a book, a picture, or some external reality or, interiorly, to some objective thought. The contemplative too, on a bad day, can fall into a daze. But this takes the form of weariness and sleep. His deepest absorption is not trancelike, but something clean and wakeful, with nothing strained or pathological about it.

Genuine contemplation involves no tension. There is no reason why it should affect anyone's nerves: on the contrary, it relaxes them. It leaves you rested and refreshed in your whole being (except perhaps where you are physically exhausted by sickness or something else). There is no strain in real contemplation, because when the gift is real, you do not depend on it, you are not enslaved by the "need" to experience anything. The contemplative does not seek reassurance in himself, in his virtue, in his state, in his "prayer." His trust is in God, not in himself. The peace and "rest" of contemplation is the fruit of a living faith in the action of divine grace. The contemplative is able to let go of himself and everything else, knowing that everything that matters in his life is in God's hands, and that he does not have to "take thought for the morrow." He fully realizes the meaning of the Gospel message of salvation by the grace of God and not by dependence on human ingenuity.

When we turn to consider the contemplative life as it is lived in cloistered orders, we run into many special psychological problems. The pressures of a rigid and institutional life are very hard even on those who are truly called to contemplation. And it is unfortunate that even in communities whose observance is supposedly designed to favor contemplation there are elements which seriously frustrate it.

The regular communal life is usually lived at the tempo of those who are active and extroverted. Impatient of interior subtleties and intolerant of all that does not bring a tangible result, these good people want to know, at the end of the day, that they have done something in the service of God. Hence their life is geared to reassure them. The day is divided up into many exercises in which prayer is measured by the clock and by the exactitude with which the ceremonial is executed. Attention is concentrated on exterior performance.

It is quite true that monastic regularity is a very important thing. But when it becomes an end in itself, it frustrates the whole purpose for which it was instituted. When attention is concentrated on externals before all else, and when there is an obsessive need to be perfect in everything (not for the glory of God, but for one's own inner peace), then true contemplation becomes impossible. For contemplation presupposes that one is free from any concern whatever, whether high or low, spiritual or material. This does not mean that carelessness and lack of discipline are more favorable to interior prayer than regular observance. Obviously, the regular life is necessary: but monastic discipline is good precisely insofar as it liberates the mind from perfectionistic concern with externals. It takes care of them, leaving one free to meditate and pray. *Evidently,*[2] then, it makes a great difference with what spirit one sets out to keep a religious rule. If regularity is a sign of love and spiritual liberty, it favors contemplation. But if it is a symptom of self-conscious and legalistic perfectionism, it kills the contemplative life at its source. And the individual who is able to rise entirely above the limitations of the community to which he belongs is a rare bird indeed.

[TWELVE]

The Desire of Contemplation

We have returned again and again to a few simple thoughts in the preceding pages: contemplative experience is something very real, but elusive and hard to define. It takes place in the depths of the subject's own spiritual being, and yet it is an "experience" of the transcendent, personal presence of God. This experience has to be carefully qualified, because its paradoxical character makes it an *experiential awareness*[1] of what cannot be experienced on earth. It is a knowledge of Him Who is beyond all knowledge. Hence, it knows Him as unknown. It knows "by unknowing."

This "dark knowledge," this "apophatic" grasp of Him Who Is, cannot be explained in a satisfactory way to anyone who has not come to experience something of the sort in his own inner life. Yet those who have felt these things easily recognize the experience in another. And the strange thing is that the phenomenon is constant. It recurs from age to age, in all kinds of places, in all kinds of societies. And its recurrence is sufficiently easy to verify empirically, as was done by William James.[2] James, as a good pragmatist, was quick to deny that he himself had entered into any of these states of consciousness. But objectively examining the claims of various mystics (perhaps without sufficient care in distinguishing the true from the false), he singled out the notes that were common to all and characterized mystical experience in each one. So, whatever may be the final value of James's research, it as least makes clear that mystical contemplation exists as an *inescapable*[3] empirical fact.

Taking a less detached view of the subject than William James and trying to see it, at least to some extent, from the inside, I have not only repeated the affirmation that contemplation is real, but I have insisted on its simplicity, sobriety, and humility and its integration in normal Christian life. This is what needs to be stressed.

No matter what we may think about the extension of the contemplative vocation (whether or not we think it is "open to all"), the fact remains that it is something "ordinary," at least de jure, in all the higher religions. For everywhere, whether in Christianity or in Buddhism, Hinduism, and Moslemism, we find examples of the contemplative life at least in a broad sense. Everywhere we find at least a natural striving for interior unity and intuitive *communion*[4] with the Absolute. And everywhere we find expressions of some kind of spiritual experience, often natural, sometimes supernatural. Supernatural mystical experience is at least theoretically possible anywhere under the sun, to any man of good conscience who sincerely seeks the truth and responds to the inspirations of divine grace.

This is of course a delicate and subtle topic, and I have not desired to enter into the fiercely debated questions which bristle around it on all sides. But it seems to me that some understanding of these facts is necessary and that the way to understand them is to see them in their simplest, and least dramatic, light. Contemplation should not be exaggerated, distorted, and made to seem great. It is essentially simple and humble. No one can enter into it except by the path of obscurity and self-forgetfulness. It implies also much discipline, but above all the normal discipline of everyday virtue. It implies justice to other people, truthfulness, hard work, unselfishness, devotion to the duties of one's state in life, obedience, charity, self-sacrifice. No one should delude himself with contemplative aspirations if he is not willing to undertake, first of all, the ordinary labors and obligations of the moral life. Contemplation is not a kind of magic and easy shortcut to happiness and perfection. And yet since it does bring one in touch with God in an I-Thou relationship of mysteriously experienced friendship, it necessarily brings that peace which Christ promised and

which "the world cannot give." There may be much desolation and suffering in the spirit of the contemplative, but there is always more joy than
sorrow, more security than doubt, more peace than desolation. The contemplative is one who has found what every man seeks in one way or other.

If that is the case, then it is surely legitimate for anyone to desire and to
seek this fulfillment, this experience of reality, this entrance into truth. But
again we stumble upon a paradox. If this desire is, in itself, legitimate, is it
nevertheless allowed to those who completely misunderstand it? Should
one be encouraged to desire contemplation if he is as yet incapable of
grasping its true nature and, still more, of fulfilling the requirements?

Let anyone desire it, provided only he is sincere and prudent and
remains open to the truth. The great obstacle to contemplation is rigidity
and prejudice. He who thinks he knows what it is beforehand prevents
himself from finding out the true nature of contemplation, since he is not
able to "change his mind" and accept something completely new. He who
thinks that contemplation is lofty and spectacular cannot receive the intuition of a supreme and transcendent Reality which is at the same time
immanent in his own ordinary self. He who needs to be exalted and for
whom mysticism is the peak of human ambition will never be able to feel
the liberation granted only to those who have renounced success. And since
most of us are rigid, attached to our own ideas, convinced of our own wisdom, proud of our own capacities, and committed to personal ambition,
contemplation is a dangerous desire for any one of us. But if we really want
to get free from these sins, the desire for contemplative freedom and for the
experience of transcendent reality is likely to arise in us all by itself, unob-
served. And it is also likely to be satisfied almost before we know we have it.
That is the way a genuine contemplative vocation is realized.

THIRTEEN

The Sense of Sin

The first step toward spiritual liberation is not so much the awareness of what lies at the end of the road—the experience of God—as a clear view of the great obstacle that blocks its very beginning. That obstacle is called sin. A great reality, a very great mystery. Both the reality and the mystery of sin seem to have become inaccessible to humanity, which now seems to be steeped in it. The hopeless "innocence" of modern man, who is so full of sin that he no longer experiences contrition and is consumed with guilt only for what is relatively inoffensive, is one of the most heartrending mysteries of our time.

The very fact that even religious people have utterly confused the concept of sin and the notion of guilt goes far to prove that we have lost all sense of the reality of sin. For sin is an interior and spiritual reality: a real evil and, in fact, the only real evil. Sin is the egg from which all other evils are hatched, and where sin is absent, any other apparent evil can be turned into good.

There is an important distinction to be made between *sin* and *guilt*. Guilt is a sense of oppression from the outside, an anxiety one feels when he thinks he is going to be called to account for a misdeed. The anxiety of guilt is a sign of moral alienation. It becomes active within us when we interiorize a reproof suggested by the presence of an authority whose edicts we have violated. The sense of guilt is, then, a sense of physical almost as much as of moral evil. I am guilty when I *think*[1] someone else believes me wrong. And the anxiety of my guilt is heightened if I secretly want to disagree with his judgment, but do not dare even to feel the disagreement.

The sense of sin is something deeper and more existential. It is not merely a sense of guilt referred to the authority of God. It is a sense of evil in myself. Not because I have violated a law outside myself, but because I have violated the inmost laws of my own being, which are, at the same time, the laws of God Who dwells within me. The sense of sin is the sense of having been deeply and deliberately false to my own inmost reality, my likeness to God. Sin is a radical evil and sickness of the spirit. Indeed, serious sin is more than that—it is the death of the spirit. To have a sense of sin is to realize myself to be not only morally but spiritually dead. Moral death would savor rather of guilt—I have been "killed" by the violation of a law. But spiritual death is the sense of having separated myself from truth by complete inner falsity, from love by selfishness, from reality by trying to assert as real a will to nothingness. The sense of sin is, then, something ontological and immediate which does not spring from reflection on my actions and comparison with a moral code. It springs directly from the evil that is present in me: it tells me not merely that I have done wrong, but that I *am* wrong, through and through. That I am a false being. That I have destroyed myself. For sin is spiritual self-destruction. And the terrible thing is that though our body dies only once, our spirit, once dead, can still be killed over and over again. To be in sin and to continue sinning is to begin the life of a soul in hell, which is perpetual and perpetually repeated death. (Remember the last scene of Sartre's *No Exit*.)[2]

The sense of sin is therefore something far deeper and more urgent than the prurient feeling of naughtiness which most pious people have trained themselves to experience when they violate the taboos of their sect. There is something scandalous about the religiosity of popular piety. All the empty gestures of people who do not do good and avoid evil, but make signs of the good, go through gesticulations which symbolize good intentions, and allay their guilt feelings with appropriate grimaces of piety. All these gestures are performed with scrupulous fidelity and accompanied with the right degree of optimism about God and man: but at the same time the most terrible of crimes are accepted without a tremor because they are, after all, collective. Take, for instance, the willingness of the majority of "believers" to accept the hydrogen bomb, with all that it implies, with no more than a shadow of theoretical protest. This is almost unbelievable, and yet it has become so commonplace that no one wonders at it anymore. The state of the world at the present day is the clearest possible indication that the whole human race is full of sin—for which responsibility becomes more and more collective and therefore more and more nebulous.

It has been remarked that the more totalitarian a society is, for example, that of Russia or of Hitler's Germany, the less its members feel any sense of sin. They can commit any evil without remorse as long as they feel they are acting as members of their collectivity. The only evil they fear is to be cut off from the community that takes their sins upon itself and "destroys" them. This is the worst of disasters, and the slightest indication of disunion with the group is the cause of anxiety and guilt.

This is the way our world is going, and in such a world the spirit and the spiritual have no more meaning because the person has no meaning. But it is the vocation and mission of the contemplative to keep alive the spirit of man, and to nurture, at least in himself, personal responsibility before God and personal independence from collective irresponsibility.

Hence *part of*[3] the mission of the contemplative is to keep alive in the world the sense of sin. In this, he is the descendent of the Old Testament prophets, for that too was their mission. They had to confront the Jewish people at every moment with the reality of sin, which cut them off from God, as distinct from ritual guilt, which could be set right with legal ceremonies. This was no pleasant vocation, because it was something more difficult and mysterious than the mere preaching of morality. Jeremias[4] had not only to teach justice and mercy, but also to persuade the people to accept the concrete will of God for them. This happened to *mean*[5] their defeat and their captivity in Babylon. The divine decree was difficult even for Jeremias to believe, and he thought himself caught at times between a deceiving God and an outraged people:

Thou hast deceived me, O Lord, and I am deceived: thou hast been stronger than I and thou hast prevailed. I am become a laughingstock all day, all scoff

at me. For I am speaking now this long time, crying out against iniquity, and
I often proclaim devastation, and the word of the Lord is made a reproach to
me, and a derision all the day. Then I said, I will not make mention of Him,
nor speak any more in His name: and there came up in my heart as a burning fire, shut up in my bones, and I was wearied, not being able to bear it.
(Jeremias 20:7–9)

The contemplative is one who is, like the servant of Yahweh,
"acquainted with infirmity," not only with his own sin, but with the sin of
the whole world, which he takes upon himself because he is a man among
men and cannot dissociate himself from the works of other men. The contemplative life in our time is therefore necessarily modified by the sins of
our age. They bring down upon us a cloud of darkness far more terrible
than the innocent night of unknowing. It is the dark night of the soul
which has descended on the whole world. Contemplation in the age of
Auschwitz[6] and Dachau,[7] Solovky[8] and Karaganda[9] is something darker
and more fearsome than contemplation in the age of the Church Fathers.

For that very reason, the urge to seek a path of spiritual light can be a
subtle temptation to sin. It certainly is sin if it means a frank rejection of
the burden of our age, an escape into unreality and spiritual illusion, so as
not to share the misery of other men.

The contemplative life today must be a life of deep sorrow and contrition, but a pure sorrow, a healing and life-giving repentance such as we
find in some of the characters of Dostoyevsky. It must be something much
deeper than the baroque and operatic sorrows of seventeenth-century
piety—the tears of El Greco saints in dark Spanish churches, against a
background of flagellants in procession. The depth of our poverty is drab
and undramatic. We have few words left in which to accept our Cross from
God. We are poorer than Job. Like him, we are tempted to curse the day
we came into existence because our whole life is full of evil. But we do
not have his eloquence. When we talk to ourselves we have even less to say
than Job's friends. We have nothing. We may spiritually share the utter
degradation of the Jews who, reduced to skeletons, walked to their death
in the furnaces of Auschwitz, but it is licit to pray to God to be spared such
extremes.

We are poor enough as it is, and our poverty includes a tacit permission to be unheroic. For this lack of show, this absence of all verve in our sacrifice, is essential to our age. There is no place in our spirituality for anything that inspires wonder, in ourselves or in others. And this is right, because man has lost all wonder for the things of God. He no longer marvels at anything except the prodigies of the Apocalyptic Beast. Hence it is right that our lives, and our prayer, should be empty of all that is wonderful. The supreme mystery is so hidden that it has nothing to show for itself at all, least of all a *Götterdämmerung,*[10] a sunset of the gods. Nietzsche, speaking for our world, proclaimed that God was dead. And that is why, in our contemplation, God must often seem to be absent, as though dead. But the truth of our contemplation is in this: that never more than today has He made His presence felt by "being absent." In this, then, we are most faithful: that we prefer the darkness and, in the very depths of our being, value this *emptiness and*[11] apparent absence. We need not struggle vainly to make Him present, if such struggles are a mockery. Leave nothingness as it is. In it, He is present.

[FOURTEEN]

Problems of the Contemplative Life

1. Contemplative Formation in Monasteries

We have seen something of the nature of the contemplative experience. And we have also briefly considered some of the mistaken tendencies in the interior life, the errors and delusions which lead us to false mysticism or to neurosis. The sense of sin, of the reality of moral and spiritual evil, is the elementary safeguard against various forms of error and falsity in the contemplative life. Without the sense of sin and the consequent understanding and acceptance of hardship, suffering, and self-sacrifice, the contemplative life will be nothing but spiritual self-indulgence, without value and without reality. All this is conveyed in simple and concrete terms by the Scriptures: "The fear of the Lord is the beginning of wisdom."[1] The fear of the Lord, the awe at the mystery of God and at the mystery of evil that stands as a wall between us and Him, is the beginning of contemplative wisdom, which lies beyond the wall. Wisdom is, in this sense, "beyond good and evil," because it is beyond the wall separating our spirit from the divine Spirit. But if one wants to be, from the very start, beyond good and evil and not know the fear of the Lord, then he can never get over the wall. It will remain insurmountable. And we will remain in the realm of confusion, of division, of good and evil: which means, in practice, subject mostly to evil.

Now we must turn to practical problems. Where can we hope to find a proper setting for contemplation? Where can we dispose ourselves in silence and detachment to learn the ways of the interior life? The answer that presents itself as the most obvious is: in some kind of monastic or contemplative community. This is logical enough. A community provides a disciplined and well-ordered way of life that is supposedly oriented toward contemplation. In such a community you will find yourself living among contemplatives, and will at least be able to see how they order their outward existence. You will, above all, receive their teaching, and one of them will be your director. Finally, and above all, the community itself is a kind of "sacrament" of the presence of God. To be in it, to participate in its life of charity and of prayer, is to live in constant union with the Holy Spirit, Who lives and acts in the community.

All this is true. This is the monastic ideal. This is the accepted theory, and there can be no doubt that it is often more or less realized even in practice. But let us remember that there will always remain something of a gap between the ideal and the real. What is juridically called a "contemplative community" may contain few or no real contemplatives. Their example may be edifying, but for a potential contemplative it may also be very misleading. The direction given may be practical and sound and may, nevertheless, be unadapted to a life of genuine contemplation. This problem was long ago discussed in detail by St. John of the Cross.

Actually, the question of the formation of real contemplatives in so-called contemplative monasteries is a complex and delicate one. I would venture to say that it is one about which very few really know anything—least of all those who have facile and simple answers to all questions on the subject.

There has been something of a monastic revival in our time. It has manifested itself everywhere in quantity and in quality. In quality, it has manifested itself mostly in Europe. Elsewhere, there have been numerous vocations and a considerable increase in the number and kind of monastic foundations. It is too early to say anything one way or the other about the quality of the monastic life in these new ventures. But certainly there does not seem to be much evidence to support the sanguine hopes of those who are going about sagely predicting that the monks are ready to fulfill, once again, the mission that was theirs in the Dark Ages. If the world is depending on *us* to carry the torch of culture through a new dark age, it is due for a disappointment.

Our modern predicament is only superficially like that which existed at the end of the Roman world, and the place of the monastery in the world is also quite different. For one thing, the monastery is no longer a new and original economic unit in society. A monastic community may be equipped to struggle through an age of chaos, but the traditional large monastery has no longer anything new or *original*[2] to contribute to society. It is an efficient, living, useful survival of the past. But it is a survival, hardly a new discovery. Innovation must come from elsewhere—for instance, from small, mobile, and detached groups like the Little Brothers of Jesus.[3]

The monastic life certainly has its place and its part to play in our modern world. The Rule of St. Benedict is a spiritual code of undying efficacy, lending itself to ever new applications in the same essential work of liturgy, labor, study, and contemplation. But monastic institutions today tend to be larger, more rigid, and more unwieldy than necessary, and it is possible that the next twenty years will see the weakening of those enormous and complex structures, in which there are so many jobs to be done that the most necessary work of all tends to be forgotten. Should potential contemplatives be urged to submit themselves to the elaborate observance of these institutions? The answer is not a simple yes or no. For a mature and well-formed person, existence in a large monastery may be the solution to many problems. It may clear the way for simple contemplation in the anonymity of communal life. But for those who are not yet formed, the factory-like action of a big community on individual souls may have a cramping effect that is ultimately harmful. It may altogether prevent a real and vital spiritual development.

The monastic life as it exists today often presupposes too much in the young postulant who seeks admission. It presupposes that he knows his own mind, that he is capable of making a mature decision, that he has grown up, that he has received a *liberal*[4] education. It is often discovered too late that such things cannot be taken for granted. Before the average youth of today is ready for monastic life, his senses, feelings, and imagination need to be reformed and educated along normal, natural lines. Americans under twenty-one who present themselves at the monastery gate are not usually full-blooded, mature men with strong passions that need to be disciplined and mortified, but confused kids with a complex bundle of vague emotional fears and desires going in all directions at once. They are a pitiful mixture of pseudo-sophistication and utter vacuity. They are not only not ready for the contemplative life, but they are not ready for any kind of life. The condition of permanently overstimulated vegetation which they have undergone for the past twenty years has disposed them for nothing except emotional breakdown at the first sight of any real moral difficulty.

Consider for instance the general atmosphere of pseudo-contemplation that pervades secular life today. The life of the television watcher is a kind of caricature of contemplation. Passivity, uncritical absorption, receptivity, inertia. Not only that, but a gradual, progressive yielding to the mystic attraction, until one is spellbound in a state of complete union. The trouble with this caricature is that it is really the exact opposite of contemplation: for true contemplation is precisely the fruit of a most active and intransigent rupture with all that captivates the senses, the emotions, and the will on a material or temporal level. The contemplative reaches his passivity only after terrific struggle with everything that appeals to his appetites as a half-animal member of the human herd. He is receptive and still only because the stillness he has reached is lucid, spiritual, and full of liberty. It is the summit of a life of personal and spiritual freedom. The other, the ersatz, is the nadir of intellectual and emotional slavery.

There is nothing in any monastic rule that foresees the arrival in a monastery of a television addict, and when he appears there, his bewilderment is scarcely less great than that of the people who become acquainted with his interior life. At first sight, he seems extremely docile, optimistic, pliable. He reacts hopefully to signs of attention. He listens to the words that are uttered in his presence and even files them away for future use himself. And he continues to wait. To wait. He is wise: he knows that what he is waiting for does not begin all at once. But it eventually begins. Perhaps after you take vows. The monastic formation is a sly game in which one gradually learns to find just one important secret: the location of the magic switch which turns on the television.

Such a one is not ready for the contemplative life because he is not ready for any kind of life. All life presupposes the ability to act, to work, to think for yourself, to break out of the cocoon, to get free from the womb. No life requires a more active or more intense formation, a more ruthless separation from dependence on exterior support, than the life of contemplation.

2. Contemplation and Technology

The problem of the contemplative life today is, then, the problem of a *natural spiritual and cultural formation* which is absolutely necessary as a basis for higher spiritual development. What we have said about "unknowing" must not be interpreted as a blanket anti-intellectualism. On the contrary, as Jacques Maritain's *Degrees of Knowledge* has made clear, the approach to God beyond concepts, in contemplation, means that one must have a conceptual knowledge beyond which he can go! There are two kinds of "unknowing"—one, the ignorance of what you do not yet know. And this is not always valid for contemplation. The other is a kind of forgetting, or transcending, of what you do know, which is proper to contemplation. This alone can be called *docta ignorantia,* or *"unknowing."* Hence the contemplative life normally presupposes a good cultural formation. And this is one of the greatest problems of the present day. Those who claim to be educated are in reality not formed: they are formless bundles of unrelated factual knowledge, disoriented and passive, superficially acquainted with names, dates, facts, and with the "how" of various material processes. But they have no way of using what they "know." Consequently, since their "knowledge" is not integrated into their lives, they cannot really be said to possess it. It has not entered into their being. It has not really become part of them.

In the preindustrial ages and in primitive societies that still exist, man is naturally prepared and disposed for contemplation. In such a world we find men who, though perhaps not all literate, possess traditional artistic and technical skills and are in a broad sense "artists" and "spiritual men."

They are formed by their tradition and their culture. Even though such men may not be able to read and write, they are not necessarily "ignorant." On the contrary, they possess a certain very important and vital kind of knowledge, and *all of it* is integrated into their lives. They have a wholeness and a humanity, and therefore a poise, a simplicity, and a confidence, which have vanished from a world in which men are alienated, enslaved to processes and to machines. Preindustrial man is therefore all ready to become a contemplative. Indeed, it can be said that in the past whole societies were oriented quite naturally to a spiritual and even contemplative life. There was no special difficulty for individuals to find their way into a monastery or to a hermitage and there devote themselves spontaneously to a life centered on the Presence and Infinite Reality of God.

Such cultures used to exist, and they may still be struggling to survive in a few places. But one can say that such cultures are doomed to disappear. One must face the fact without bitterness and without useless nostalgia for the past. Times have changed, and man has changed with them. But he is always man, and as long as he has a human nature, human freedom, human personality, he is the image of God, and is consequently capable of using his love and freedom in the highest of all his activities—in contemplation. But, as I say, times have changed, and in the education of modern man the fact that he is the image of God does not carry much weight. Indeed, nothing could be treated with less concern *today*[5] than man's innate capacity to be a contemplative.

The modern child may in the beginning of his conscious life begin to show natural and spontaneous signs of spirituality. He may have imagination, originality, a simple and individual freshness of response to reality, and even a tendency to moments of thoughtful silence and absorption. But all these qualities are quickly destroyed by the fears, anxieties, and compulsions to conform which come at him from all directions. He becomes a yelling, brash, false little monster, brandishing a toy gun and dressed up like some character he has seen on television. His head is filled with inane slogans, songs, noises, explosions, statistics, brand names, menaces, ribaldries, and clichés. When he gets to school he learns to verbalize, to rationalize, to pose, to make faces like an advertisement, to need a car, and in short to go through life with an empty head, conforming to others like himself, *in "togetherness."*[6]

He may be in some sense educated, but his education has little to do with real life, since real life is not something with which modern man is really concerned at all. The conscious life of modern man is completely lost in intellectual abstractions, sensual fantasies, political, social, and economic clichés, and in the animal cunning of the detective or the salesman. All that is potentially valuable and vital in him is relegated to the subconscious mind: and sex is not what he most tends to suppress. The tragedy of modern man is that his creativity, his spirituality, and his contemplative independence are inexorably throttled by a superego that has sold itself without question or compromise to the devil of technology.

Notice that this mentality existed also in the past, in the magician and the medicine man, in the astrologer, the alchemist, and the witch. These too were spiritual monsters who entered into a Faustian pact with evil and immolated their creative freedom, their contemplative innocence, on the altar of power. These men were the true ancestors of the modern technological bureaucrat: the man who wants nothing but to *control* things, and to manipulate people as objects. In the old days the Faust pact worked for only a few because society was healthy. Today it works for millions: we live in a Faustian world.

There is of course a considerable morbid interest in "the soul" today, even though the soul's existence is denied. Writers, for instance, have been called "engineers of the human soul" and that by one of the greatest and most pompous of our Fausts—and one of our most pontifical atheists. Modern man is, then, interested in the soul as something *he*[7] can control in somebody else. It is something over which *he* can exercise power. It is a kind of spiritual "handle" by which *he* can seize another person and turn him into an instrument. This is the exact opposite of the contemplative approach. The contemplative seeks to liberate his soul from all external control, to purify and detach it from material, sensual, and even spiritual compulsions, and to surrender it to the truth and creative freedom of the Holy Spirit. And in liberating himself, he becomes able to show others the way to the same liberty, because his life bears witness to a supreme liberty and enables them to know it, obscurely, and to burn with its desire.

The education of a technological bureaucrat is, then, the exact opposite to what is required for a contemplative. Yet there may exist a surprising contemplative temptation in the heart of modern man: a temptation that arises with a certain facility when he apprehends the contemplative experience as a source of power.

With what does popular religion seek to beguile modern man? With the promise of spiritual power. Religion is put forward as something superior to technology, for God the supreme technocrat is behind it all and running the whole business. So you get in with the big Boss, the Chief upstairs in his office on the top floor of the Babel National Bank. And He will see to it that you are a success. He will give you contemplation—spiritual *power*, a kind of invulnerability, a magic perfection. You become infallible, at least in your own private life. You open the door to an inner room in which you can't be wrong and which no one can enter in order to find fault with you. That is a certain, enviable, schizophrenic kind of power. But the trouble with it is that it is characteristically magic and has nothing spiritual about it. It has nothing to do with contemplation. It simply enables you to defend yourself in a world where other technocrats are trying to get hold of you and rule you through your "soul."

3. *Preparation for the Contemplative Life*

The problem of contemplation for the average modern man is, then, a problem of *preparation*. The average man of our time is disposed to be a contemplative in reverse, a mystic of technocracy or of business. His contemplation will be a pragmatic affair, something eminently worthwhile which, if you go about it by the approved and latest methods, will bring quick results. And here psychological self-analysis comes in: indeed, maybe a battery of tests will help you find out whether or not you have a contemplative vocation. In any case, you have to watch yourself and your complexes.

It is true that analytical psychology has something to say about the peripheral accidents of the interior life. But if one thinks that the accretion of one more technique will do the trick, he is badly mistaken. It may do nothing but increase the already disastrous confusion.

Let us consider what was said above about man in the past. This will give us some idea of the proper preparation that the contemplative life requires. A life that is quiet, lived in the country, in touch with the rhythm of nature and the seasons. A life in which there is manual work, the exercise of arts and skills, not in a spirit of dilettantism, but with genuine reference to the needs of one's existence. The cultivation of the land, the care of farm animals, gardening. A broad and serious literary culture, music, art: again not in the spirit of *Time* and *Life*—(a chatty introduction to *Titian*,[8] *Praxiteles*,[9] and Jackson Pollock[10])—but a genuine and creative appreciation of the way poems, pictures, etc., are *made*. A life in which there is such a thing as serious conversation, and little or no TV. These things are mentioned not with the insistence that *only* life in the country can prepare a man for contemplation, but to show the type of exercise that is needed.

When I say this prepares one for the contemplative life, I do not necessarily mean that one goes from there to a monastery. But it is a question that large monasteries might consider. To receive an unprepared postulant, fresh from high school or college, directly into the organized routine of the monastic life is, eight times out of ten,[11] to take in a transient guest who will board in the novitiate for three months or six and then go home in deep distress. But this is not what novitiates are for.

The large monasteries are worlds in themselves, institutions of great and impersonal size, busy and complex, in which each member tends to become a cog in a machine. True, it may be a contemplative machine. But we are no longer in the Middle Ages, and though the monastic life may have a theoretically medieval pattern, its tempo is often that of the factory or the house of business. There is none of the seemingly aimless leisure, the thoughtlessness of time which the contemplative life requires. There is of course a certain culture—indeed, it may be quite a deep culture: liturgical, historical, spiritual, theological, mystical. Yet inevitably the monastic library tends to imitate the library of a university, and some of the monks become graduate students doing research. They are busy, if not with a thesis, at least with a project. This is good, even in some cases necessary. But again, it is not the tempo of contemplation. There is of course the liturgy. Needless to say, that is probably the biggest project of all, a huge, worried, complicated, time-devouring project, mobilizing the ceaseless concern of experts in chant and the anxiety of every monk in the community, whether he can sing or not. There is manual work, of course, but it is impersonal, proletarian. There may be a complete absence of individual responsibility, or such an aggregation of responsibilities that one cracks under them. The Bible is read, but it is full of mysteries which remain to be unveiled by an expert with a degree; and he, too often, is interested only in details of archeology and linguistics.

All these things have been said soberly, certainly with something more than compassion, since I describe a situation which is acutely familiar to me. To say them is not to criticize or to complain. Such developments are inevitable. I *refuse to*[12] quarrel with those who think them desirable.

The large monastery can safely and efficiently absorb two kinds of people. First, it can take those who are spiritually mature and already disposed to be contemplatives; it can give them a well-ordered or at least systematic existence that is secure, devout, and even sporadically silent. Such men can live contented lives in the anonymity of their surroundings and can develop into true contemplatives. Second, the monastery can also take men who are not called to be contemplatives in the *full*[13] sense of the word, but who need a strict and organized community life full of "religious exercises" which will teach them a certain kind of asceticism and remind them to keep practicing it. These are the juridical contemplatives who are called contemplatives because they live in a "contemplative monastery" and follow its exercises. They are quite content, feeling no further need of anything more intimate and personal. The last thing that occupies their mind is the dangerously ambiguous proposition that one can have a "quasi-experiential knowledge of God in obscurity." They can get along very well without the "cloud of unknowing," and for the talk about the divine light as a "ray of darkness" they feel nothing but contempt. God is in His heaven; His liturgy is carried out on earth. The great thing is to sing loud, observe the rubrics, and beg God seven times in the day to punish Communists. These are the types who normally preponderate in "contemplative" communities.

Here, then, is the difficulty. The large monastic community can offer a fruitful, meaningful life to anyone who is already mature and ready for "contemplation," whether real or merely juridical. But if monastic orders are going to prepare undeveloped postulants and give them enough formation and natural maturity to enter a contemplative novitiate, they are going to have to make room for something new. There will have to be quiet, separate communities of postulants in which not only an elementary religious formation is imparted, but also a thorough psychological, cultural, and generally *human* training. And of course the very first thing about this training will have to be its basic difference from training in secular colleges. There the student passively receives material which has previously been thought out and digested for him. Here the postulant is going to occupy himself not with facts, or even skills—though he may have to learn the Latin he needs. He is going to learn to go through normal human experiences and be aware of them and of himself with a certain amount of depth. He is going to learn to be alone with himself and with his thoughts. To sit still. To work at making something.

These things cannot be taken care of in a novitiate. There, fasting, work, silence, meditation, prayer, and liturgy are all matters of rule and discipline. One practices them under relative tension, in an atmosphere of critical uncertainty. One is being "put to the test." But one is not ready for these projects under trying conditions unless he has first experienced them in a relaxed and precisely untrying atmosphere. What is the use of "mortifying" your senses before you have had the pleasure of using them normally and innocently in the enjoyment of the good things of nature: before you have learned to *see* with your eyes, *taste* with your tongue, and *experience* reality with your whole being? One must first learn to make a leisurely comparison between the feeling of gratitude for a simple meal and the *liberation and relief*[14] of being empty on a fast day. One must compare the pleasure of sensible conversation with the equal pleasure of being silent and alone with one's own thoughts. One must know the satisfaction of doing good and productive manual work as well as the discipline of boring and even useless tasks performed under obedience. If the men who entered monasteries had all received this kind of well-rounded and harmonious preformation, they would in consequence not *manifest*[15] so many eccentric, strange, and warped interpretations of monastic observance.

In the small monastic community, where a Superior with broad views and deep understanding of human problems can adjust the tempo of life for the best interests of all his monks, this kind of preformation can be carried out during a long postulancy in the community itself, because the person of the postulant will continue to be a matter of importance to all.

In the large community, though one or two may have the postulant's interests at heart and try to do something for him, he will eventually be carried away by the irresponsible arbitrariness of the institutional spirit.

It is instructive to study the small Carmelite communities instituted by St. Teresa of Avila and St. John of the Cross for the express purpose of forming contemplatives. First, they were always to remain small and select. Twenty was already too big. *Twenty-two was the outside limit.*[16] The discipline was strict and was well kept. But the understanding of observance was always broad and intelligent. The Superior was something more than an official. Prayer was taken very seriously, along with penance, silence, solitude, fasting, and work. But human values were not forgotten, and when it came to a conflict between human values and prayer, St. Teresa favored the former. To be convinced of this we have only to read the long chapter (VI) in the *Book of Foundations,* in which she shows how those who have been led into exaggerations and delusions in their way of prayer are to deliberately distract themselves from what seems to them to be spiritual, in order to keep in touch with the ordinary human realities of life. Recreations in St. Teresa's Carmels were always gay, and the saint herself sang, danced, and played the lute. St. John of the Cross took his friars out to meditate in the mountains and loved to talk with them of God in the beauties of nature. St. Teresa so valued intelligence and human balance that she said she would be willing to see the rule relaxed at any time in favor of a good theologian who wanted to become a Carmelite friar, if that would help him adjust to his new life.

4. Contemplative Life in the World

We have given close attention to some of the problems of contemplative life in a monastery, the chief of them growing out of the rigidly institutional character of the monastic life today. At the other extreme, we have the isolated layman trying to keep up an interior life "in the world" without the support of any institutional structure and without any defense against the pressures and distractions of secular life.

Writers who concerned themselves in the past with the spiritual life had their own standard appreciation of "the world." The conflict between the world and God, in the heart of the man of prayer, traditionally took the form of a tug of war between the allurements of a life of pleasure, full of joy and satisfaction, and the stern pull of duty drawing him on to sacrifice, austerity, and peace in God. Today the situation has changed; the temptation is different, less lusty and infinitely more grim.

Even those whom the clichés of an earlier time might have called the "votaries of the world" have lost all sense of satisfaction in their devotion to a tyrannical master. Solitude and silence, essential to the contemplative life, have become highly valued luxuries sometimes accessible only to the rich. Peace, which exists nowhere except in dreams, haunts the waking hours of those whose life is a despairing struggle for security. The contemplative monk is quite likely to be the object of the worldling's envy— which was not necessarily true in the past. The monk has his sacrifices and his rule: but the rule of the world, its exacting demands, its inexorable pressures to conform, is clearly much harder than that. Not only does the world become more and more demanding, but it *cannot* be escaped. There are still islands, mountains, and deserts to which a few privileged individuals can make their way. But even these are more and more rapidly being invaded—just like the monasteries themselves. One of the great problems of the contemplative life today is the necessity to adapt to an unsatisfactory situation and make the best of it. This is true inside the monastery as well as outside it.

The truth is that everyone would like to escape from the pressures, the anguish, the insecurity, and the peril of secular life, but that no one can do without the benefits that are inseparably connected with these pressures. The paradox of the truly monastic vocation today is the paradox of a desire for peace that is strong enough to resist and break away from the conflicts of the world, for it is by conflict that the world holds us. And duty nowadays always seems to turn up on the side where there is the most conflict. One feels guilty in renouncing the struggles of secular life, as if one had some kind of obligation to go on accepting an existence in which the spirit is exhausted and frustrated, as if one could not in conscience allow himself to find real peace. And where the conflicts and contradictions of secular life find their way into a busy monastery, they suddenly by some miracle cease to be secular and become religious: business affairs and material preoccupations are now "the cross" and to sidestep them is regarded as infidelity.

This is no simple question, because obviously community life has its material obligations, and because outside the monastery the spiritual life of the average Christian is dominated by this same struggle. Nevertheless, it seems right to say that one who wants a contemplative life today, whether he is in a monastery or in the world, must do two things. First, he must as far as possible reduce the conflict and frustration in his life by cutting down his contact with the "world" and his secular subjections. This means reducing his needs for pleasure, comfort, recreation, prestige, and success and embracing a life of true spiritual poverty and detachment. Second, he must learn to put up with the inevitable conflicts that remain—the noise, the agitation, the crowding, the lack of time, and above all the constant contact with a purely secular mentality which is all around us everywhere and at all times, even to some extent in monasteries.

Now if it is hard to prepare for a contemplative life even in a monastery, how much harder will it be outside one? It can be truly said that for very many people for this reason the contemplative life is simply out of the question. For others, only a minor miracle (which they are perfectly entitled to pray for) can bring about a change of conditions that would make such a life possible. Even for those best endowed and prepared, the ordinary conditions of urban life today are so inimical to spirituality that they will have to keep up a ceaseless struggle if they are to enjoy even the most elementary kind of interior life. Only the exceptional man [or woman],[17] left to himself, will be able to live on a deep enough level to prevent his spirituality from being completely blown away; or, to put it in better terms, to keep himself free from the collective pressures and dictates which keep him in subjection to the spirit of the world and render him insensitive to the Spirit of God.

It would seem that for this reason groups of laypeople interested in the spiritual life should be formed in order to protect and foster something of an elementary contemplative spirituality. Obviously the already existing movements interested in liturgy and the study of the Scriptures could help in this direction. It is strange that contemplative monasteries are content simply to receive individuals as retreatants, encourage them to receive frequent Communion and make the Way of the Cross, but do not do more to form groups of men who could help and support one another. One thinks, for instance, of a kind of contemplative Third Order, connected with the Cistercians or the Carthusians. But as soon as you start thinking in terms of organization, the issue becomes extremely confused. Such groups do not need to be *organized*. They simply need to form themselves, under the guidance and encouragement of priests who are already interested in contemplation.

These groups could provide their members with books, conferences, direction, and perhaps a quiet place in the country where they could go for a few days of meditation and prayer. Here a little originality and initiative might be encouraged. Christian laypeople are often too passively dependent on the spiritual initiatives of their clergy and tend to think that there is no form of spiritual retreat other than the conventional meetings, with routine exercises, held in monasteries.

If you are waiting for someone to come along and feed you the contemplative life with a spoon, you are going to wait a long time, especially in America. You had better renounce your inertia, pray for a little imagination, ask the Lord to awaken your creative freedom, and consider some of the following possibilities:

1. It is possible that by the sacrifice of seemingly good economic opportunities, you could move into the country or to a small town where you would have more time to think. This would involve the acceptance of a relative poverty perhaps. If so, all the better for your interior life. The sacrifice could be a real liberation from the pitiless struggle which is the source of most of your worries. There are of course jobs which by their nature keep one isolated or take him off the beaten track. However, not everyone is free to choose the career of forest ranger or lighthouse keeper. Not everybody wants to spend his life as a night watchman, and for very good reasons. But what is wrong with farming?

2. Wherever you may be, it is always possible to give yourself the benefit of those parts of the day which are quiet because the world does not value them. One of these is the small hours of the morning. Even when a man cannot put a few hundred miles between himself and the city, if he can get up around four or five in the morning, he will have the whole

place to himself and taste something of the peace of solitude. Besides, the dawn is by its very nature a peaceful, mysterious, and contemplative time of day—a time when one naturally pauses and looks with awe at the eastern sky. It is a time of new life, new beginning, and therefore important to the spiritual life: for the spiritual life is nothing else but a perpetual interior renewal. To go to early Mass is always preferable, even though the later Masses may be more splendid and solemn. At the early Mass, things are quieter, more sober, more austere. The poor go to early Mass because they have to get to work sooner. And Christ is more truly with the poor. His spiritual presence among them makes *their* Mass the more contemplative one.

3. It should be too obvious to mention that Sunday is set apart by nature and by the tradition of the Church as a day of contemplation. Puritan custom tended to make Sunday seem a negative sort of "Sabbath" characterized most of all by the things one "must not" do. The inevitable reaction against this stressed the legitimate, but more or less insignificant, recreations that make Sunday a day of rest for the body as well as for the spirit. Obviously, if you sleep all Sunday morning you are missing something about the day of rest that is more important than bodily sleep. Sunday is a day of contemplation not because it is a day without work, a day when the shops and banks and offices are closed, but because it is sacred to the mystery of the Resurrection. Sunday is the "Lord's Day" not in the sense that, on one day out of the week, one must stop and think of Him, but because it breaks into the ceaseless, "secular" round of time with a burst of light out of a sacred eternity. We stop working and rushing about on Sunday not only in order to rest up and start over again on Monday, but in order to collect our wits and realize the relative meaninglessness of *the secular business which fills*[18] the other six days of the week, and taste the satisfaction of a peace which surpasses understanding and which is given us by Christ. *Sunday reminds us of the peace that should filter through the whole week when our work is properly oriented.*[19]

Sunday is a contemplative day not just because Church Law demands that every Christian assist at Mass, but because everyone, Christian or not, who celebrates the day spiritually, and accepts it at its face value, opens his heart to the light of Christ, the light of the Resurrection. In doing so he grows in love, in faith, and is able to "see" a little more of the mystery of Christ. He certainly may have no clear idea of what is happening, but the grace of God produces its effects in his heart. Sunday, then, is a day of grace, a day of light, in which light is given. Simple fidelity to this obvious duty, realization of this gift of God, will certainly help the harassed layman to take his first steps on the path to a kind of contemplation.

4. Wherever one seeks the light of contemplation, he commits himself by that very fact to a certain spiritual discipline. This is just as true outside the cloister as in it. But it would be a mistake for a man or woman with all the obligations and hardships of secular life to live in the world like a cloistered monk. To try to do this would be an illusion. The first sacrifice of the lay contemplative living in the world is his acceptance of the fact that he is *not* a monk and, consequently, of the fact that his prayer life must be correspondingly humble and poor. Active virtue and good works play a large part in the "contemplative" life that is led in the world, and the uncloistered man of prayer is most likely to be what we have called a "masked contemplative." It will only do him harm if, tormented by his thirst for a clearer and higher experience, he tries to force the issue and advance his "degree of prayer" by violent and ill-considered efforts.

The discipline of the contemplative in the world is first of all the discipline of fidelity to his duty of state—to his obligations as head of a family, as a member of a profession, as a citizen. This discipline, these duties can demand very great sacrifices. Perhaps, indeed, some of the difficulties of people in the world exact of them far greater sacrifice than they would find in the cloister. In any case, their contemplative life will be deepened and elevated by the depth of their understanding and their duties. Here too, mere conformism and lip service are not enough. It is not sufficient to "be a good Catholic." One must penetrate the inner meaning of his life in Christ and see the full significance of its demands. One must carry out his obligations not as a question of form, but with a real, personal decision to offer the good he does to God, in and through Christ. The virtue of a Christian is something creative and spiritual, not simply a fulfillment of a law. It must be penetrated and filled with the "newness," the Christlikeness, which comes from the action of the Spirit of God in his heart, and which elevates his smallest good act to an entirely spiritual level.

Needless to say, this is more than a matter of verbalizing one's "purity of intention."

5. It follows from this that for the married Christian, his married life is essentially bound up with his contemplation. This is inevitable. It is by his marriage that he is situated in the mystery of Christ. It is by his marriage that he bears witness to Christ's love for the world, and in his marriage that he experiences that love. His marriage is a sacramental center from which grace radiates out into every department of his life, and consequently it is his marriage that will enable his work, his leisure, his sacrifices, and even his distractions to become in some degree contemplative. For by his marriage all these things are ordered to Christ and centered in Christ. It should above all be emphasized that for the married Christian, even and especially married love enters into his contemplation, and this, as a matter of fact, gives it a special character.

The union of man and wife in nuptial love is a sacred and symbolic act, the very nature of which signifies the mystery of the union of God and man in Christ. Now this mystery is the very heart and substance of contemplation. Hence, married love is a kind of material and symbolic expression of man's desire for God and God's desire for man. It is a blind, simple, groping way of expressing man's need to be utterly and completely *one*. It is a childlike acting out of division of man in himself and of his hunger for union with his other self. The Greek Fathers thought that before the Fall Adam and Eve were really and literally two *in one flesh,* that is to say, they were one single *being*.[20] That human nature, united with God, was whole and complete in itself. But after the Fall man was divided into two and thereafter sought by sexual love to recover his lost unity. But this desire is ever frustrated by original sin. The fruit of sexual love is not perfection, not completeness, but only the birth of another Adam or another Eve, frail, exiled, incomplete. The child in turn grows to manhood, and, devoured by the old yearning for completeness, marries, reiterates the dark mystery of love and hopelessness, brings forth new beings to incompleteness and frustration, and finally dies incomplete.

But the coming of Christ has exorcised the futility and despair of the children of Adam. Christ has married human nature, united man and God in Himself, in one Person. In Christ, the completeness we were born for is realized. In Him there is no longer marrying or giving in marriage. But in Him all are one in the perfection of charity.

Pius XII pointed out in the encyclical *Sacra Virginitas* that the state of Christian virginity, with its pure love attaining to contemplation, lays hold on the reality and substance of that union with God which married love imperfectly attempts to symbolize. Therefore the virginal state is more perfect, because contemplation is more germane to it, and theoretically inseparable from it. However, married love, in its more humble and more earthy way may in fact be, for the enlightened layman, a more concrete and sensible approach to the great mystery. He lays hold on his lost unity in that secret mystery of sorrow and ecstasy, humiliation and joy, triumph and death, which is his own peculiar participation in the mystery of Christ.

Hence it is clear that for the married Christian layman, contemplation does not involve the disciplines and attitudes proper to a virgin. The married Christian should beware of letting himself be influenced too much by a virginal or priestly spirituality that has nothing to do with his state and only blinds him to its essential dignity. There are in fact too many books which look at the spiritual life exclusively from the standpoint of a virginal or priestly life, and their needless multiplication is, in fact, the reason why there is so much sterile spiritual writing. At the same time, this sterile influence makes itself felt in the interior life of those married Christians who should have the greatest influence for good in keeping the Christian mind fully and sanely *incarnate*.

In conclusion, then, though it is right that the Christian layman try to keep his life ordered and peaceful, and to some extent recollected, what he needs most of all is a contemplative spirituality centered in the mystery of marriage. The development of such a spirituality is very necessary and much to be desired.

FIFTEEN

Prospects and Conclusions

The most significant development of the contemplative life "in the world" is the growth of small groups of men and women who live in every way like the laypeople around them, except for the fact that they are dedicated to God and focus all their life of work and poverty upon a contemplative center. Such is the life of the fraternities of the Little Brothers of Jesus,[1] the most typical of twentieth-century innovations in the contemplative life. The Little Brothers do not form a religious order in the strict sense of the word. They have no special religious habit; they do not live in enclosed monasteries. Though some of them are priests, they do not exercise a formal apostolic ministry among the faithful, do not have parishes or missions. Priests and Brothers alike wear ordinary civilian clothing and work at ordinary jobs, in factories or on farms, availing themselves of the normal opportunities for work open to the poor among whom they live. They seek to imitate the hidden life of Jesus Christ at Nazareth, where He was a common workman undistinguishable from the others around Him in the small Galilean town.

The fraternities of the Little Brothers are houses or apartments in the poor districts of cities or cabins in poverty-stricken country areas. The only thing that distinguishes them from any other worker's dwelling is the fact that there is an altar, a tabernacle, and the Blessed Sacrament. This altar in the home is the center of the contemplative life of the fraternity. Mass is offered there daily before a congregation of ten or a dozen worshipers, usually only the Brothers themselves. The Blessed Sacrament is the Living Heart of this contemplative life. The Brothers spend as much of their free time as they can in silent adoration before the tabernacle, during the day or night. Naturally, as their General, Fr. René Voillaume, has pointed out, they must expect and fully accept poverty in their contemplation also. Theirs is the life of the poor in every respect. Theirs must also be the prayer of the poor. Hence, distractions, fatigue, incapacity to meditate, lack of sensible fervor, disorientation, weakness, and even apparent failure. But a few words on this subject from the pen of René Voillaume should be quoted here. They will throw light on what was said above about masked contemplation, and will encourage all those whose life of prayer is seriously handicapped by the tempo of work or the pressure of other duties in modern life. Fr. Voillaume asks:

How are you to meet the conditions requisite to authentic prayer in working life, and how are you to go about engaging in it generously? Such is your constant concern. You may even, at moments, have believed it impossible. Face to face with the problem in all its gravity, I confess that I too have felt at times as if at the starting point of an unfamiliar and terrible dangerous and narrow road. I have questioned whether I had any right to urge you upon it. . . . But I knew I could not do otherwise. . . . The steepest roads are often the best and quickest. The traveler is less inclined to loiter on the way up. . . . When the time comes for prayer, we shall the more often be incapable of meditating, incapable of really thinking. There must be some other way for us to join God in prayer. . . . The way we must go to God is to go to Him with our entire beings, as best we can . . . we are carried to Him by the living faith, the living hope and the living charity in us. Here you are going to need a great deal of courage. You must therefore know that acts of these virtues are in no way dependent upon the sensible or consoling impressions we may have of them. It is enough to know that we *are* sons of God and to be certain that we *will* to give ourselves to Him. The better part of ourselves is not the one we can feel. (*Seeds of the Desert*, pp. 187–89)

There is nothing of quietism in this. It is an arid, austere, difficult way of prayer. It brings the solitude and dryness of the desert into the cities, where men are obsessed with pleasure and money, and with diversion. It is a redemptive, silent, and humble prayer which keeps Christ present, in a special way, hidden in human society atoning for its sins. The followers of Charles de Foucauld[2] have no special pastoral task allotted to them. They do not argue with people, try to convince them, try to convert them, try to make them amend their lives. They seek only to *be* with them, to share their lives, their poverty, their sufferings, their problems, their ideals: but to be with them in a special way. As members of Christ, they *are* Christ. And where they are present, Christ is present. Where He is present, He acts. Their being, their presence, is then active, dynamic. It is the leaven hidden in the measure of meal. This of course is a strictly contemplative view of the Christian life, and unless it implies a complete sacrifice of oneself, of all one's ambitions and worldly desires, it cannot be effective. But once it is properly understood, it is utterly simple. So much so, that it is terrible in its simplicity. It is the simplicity of the Gospel itself.

The ideal of the Little Brothers was discovered and lived at the beginning of our century by Charles de Foucauld, a former French army officer and explorer who was converted from a worldly life, entered a Trappist monastery, and then left it to live as a hermit in the Sahara desert. When he was a Trappist, everyone who knew him was edified by his austerity and by his prayer. But after he left the Order, many apparently lost the ability to understand his further development. The contemplative orders, in general, are mystified by Charles de Foucauld and have a distinct tendency to leave him alone. They cannot be sure whether or not he is a traitor to the cause. His canonization is being promoted in Rome by the White Fathers, who are African missionaries.

Among professional and normal contemplative groups, there seem to be grave doubts that the life led by Charles de Foucauld was "contemplative." He was not in a monastery. He followed a strange personal inspiration of his own instead of keeping with an accepted institution. He lived among the Tuaregs[3] (whom he had selected as the poorest and most abandoned people on the face of the earth). He talked with them, studied their language, tried to help them economically as well as spiritually. In short, his formula for the "contemplative" life seems simply to have been to go off into the desert and become, for all practical purposes, a Tuareg.

If this formula seems at first sight to be disconcerting, it is because we have too narrow and rigid an idea of the contemplative life. Perhaps we emphasize too much the things that the contemplative life is not. We draw up lists of restrictions and assume that no life can be called contemplative unless it includes these restrictions: separation from the world, silence, physical solitude, monastic enclosure, no pastoral ministry, etc. It is perfectly true that all these restrictions ideally favor the development of an interior and contemplative life. But perhaps we are concerned too much with these restrictions as juridical postulates, as legalities, in their existence on paper. Certainly it should be clear that a man who leaves a highly developed, sophisticated, and wealthy society in order to live among poor and primitive people in a desert has certainly left "the world" much more truly and completely than one who, remaining in his civilized society, has entered one of its wealthy, comfortable, mechanized, and highly respected monasteries.

Tuaregs are technically "civilians" or *"seculars"*[4] while the monks of the monastery back home are "religious"; and certainly a Tuareg settlement is not a monastic enclosure. But if we pause to consider that the first monks of all, the Egyptian Desert Fathers, the pioneers of the monastic and contemplative lives, were *laypeople,* and were, furthermore, very much like the Tuaregs, and led very much the same kind of life that Charles de Foucauld led in the Hoggar,[5] then we will have to somewhat revise our hasty judgments.

Even more interesting and important than the ideal of Charles de Foucauld is that of the rare spirits like the late Father Monchanin[6] who have attempted to bring the deepest and truest Christian contemplation into contact with the mysticism of the Orient. Here we can see more clearly than anywhere else the contrast between the big, "official" contemplative institutions and the small, vital, and original contemplative groups that are beginning to emerge as characteristic of our time.

The contemplative life began to break into the missions at the end of the nineteenth century with characteristic virtues and defects. It is amazing to see how the conception has begun to change (though the old idea is still prevalent almost everywhere). The first contemplative monasteries in "mission lands" were blatantly "colonial." No one, it seemed, was capable of planning anything else. From a large, prosperous "motherhouse" in Europe there came a colony of monks, men of their country and of their time, with little understanding of the alien culture into which they were being transplanted. Their function was to set up a "dynamo of prayer" in the midst of the "darkness of paganism." They were dimly aware that these "pagans" had something of a spiritual doctrine, but of course it was "all dreams." The Buddhist sought to exterminate himself in *nirvana* and the yogi tried to produce ecstasies by self-hypnosis. All this was too degraded or absurd to merit attention: one simply prayed that the light of God would get through to these benighted minds.

In order to accomplish this, one built a huge, elaborate replica of the motherhouse in Europe. One *carefully preserved*[7] all the European ways of living, customs, clothing, and furniture, and one strove to impose with minute exactitude all the slightest regulations and observances that had been imported from the motherhouse. Hence the contemplative mon-astery in the Orient was a missionary branch office of the big mother-house in Europe, and the *"native"*[8] vocations who entered the monastery became pseudo-Europeans at the same time as they became monks. It would be wrong to say that the sincerity and efficacy of the monastic life itself did not bring about a genuine spiritual contact. Such monasteries bore real fruit. But not nearly enough fruit. And they were, it seems, fore-doomed to immediate extinction once the hated colonial powers were driven out of the country.

Father Monchanin, on the contrary, was a French secular priest who went with a companion into southern India. There, dressed in the familiar robe of a Hindu monk, he formed a Christian *ashram*, a monastery of simple huts, without chairs, tables, or European furniture. The daily round of prayer was not based purely on the European pattern, but corresponded more to oriental custom. Father Monchanin had made a study of Hindu-ism and of Indian mysticism, and his *ashram* was not a branch office of anything in the West. It was a humble and genuine venture in the con-templative life, not for the sake of extending a monastic institution, but in order to get closer to the truth. Contemplation in this sense reaches out beyond the boundaries of Western civilization and, in the spirit of those great saints of the past who sought to incorporate into Christianity what was good in the philosophy of Greece, seeks also what may be germane to the Gospel in the superabundant richness of oriental mysticism.

Once again, we see clearly that the contemplative life is much more than a life in which one does not see, think about, notice, or attend to what goes on "outside the monastery." A contemplative is not just a man who stays apart from other men and meditates while they struggle to make their living. He is not just a man who forgets about the world, with its political or cultural upheavals, and sits absorbed in prayer while bombers swarm in the air over his monastery. Most of the trouble with the contemplative life today comes from this purely negative approach.

The contemplative life is primarily a life of *unity*. A contemplative is one who has transcended divisions to reach a unity beyond division. It is true that he must begin by separating himself from the ordinary activities of men to some extent. He must recollect himself, turn within, in order to find the inner center of spiritual activity which remains inaccessible as long as he is immersed in the exterior business of life. But once he has found this center, it is very important that he realizes what comes next.

Very many frustrated contemplatives are people who have managed to break away from exterior distractions and to find their way to the spiritual center of their being. They have become momentarily aware of God and of the possibilities of the contemplative life. But they have imagined that the way to live it was to sit still, curled up upon themselves, coddling the inner experience which they had discovered. This is a fatal misconception. First of all, it isolates the contemplative within himself and cuts him off from all other realities. But in this way he becomes engrossed and absorbed in himself. His introversion leads to a kind of torpid imprisonment in himself, and this, of course, is the ruin of all true contemplation.

Contemplation must not be confused with abstraction. A contemplative life is not to be lived by permanent withdrawal within one's own mind. The diminished and limited existence of a small, isolated, specialized group is not enough for "contemplation." The true contemplative is not less interested than others in normal life, not less concerned with what goes on in the world, but *more* interested, more concerned. The fact that he is a contemplative makes him capable of a greater interest and of a deeper concern. Since he is detached, since he has received the gift of a pure heart, he is not limited to narrow and provincial views. He is not easily involved in the superficial confusion which most men take for reality. And for that reason he can see more clearly and enter more directly into the pure actuality of human life. The thing that distinguishes him from other men, and gives him a distinct advantage over them, is that he has a much more spiritual grasp of what is "real" and what is "actual."

This does not mean that the contemplative mind has a deeper practical insight into political or economic affairs. Nor that the contemplative can beat the mathematician and engineer at their own games. In all that seems most practical and urgent to other men, the contemplative may distinguish himself perhaps only by ineptitude and near folly. But he still has the inestimable gift of appreciating, at their real worth, values that are permanent, authentically deep, human, truly spiritual, and even divine.

This means that the contemplative is not simply a specialist in a certain esoteric spiritual field. If he is no more than this, he has failed in his vocation. No, his mission is to be a complete and whole man, with an instinctive and generous need to further the same wholeness in others and in all mankind. He arrives at this, however, not by superior gifts and special talents, but by the simplicity and poverty which are essential to his state because they alone keep him traveling in the way that is spiritual, divine, and beyond understanding.

He is the one who is best attuned to the logos of man's present situation, immersed in its mystery, acquainted with its deepest suffering, and sensitive to its most viable hopes. He is the one who is in harmony with the Tao. Hence he cannot help but look at the world attentively and with much more understanding than the politician who thinks himself in command. The contemplative knows who is in command, and knows whom to obey, though he does not always understand the commands any more than others do.

There was, at least for a time, an element of pseudo-gnosticism in the Marxist contemplation of history: in the belief that those fully initiated into the mystery of dialectics could find the mysterious and dynamic force central to history and by their discovery come to control it. Or, if you prefer, that man could come to discover himself in discovering the dialectical development of history and by consciously entering into a communion with history that would gradually turn into control. There is something exciting in this temptation because, in its pure form, such gnosticism is relatively noble. (Contrast it with the brutal degeneracy of the Stalinist line in power politics.) But it savors of illuminism and of magic. It is, in reality, *an arbitrary*[9] and eclectic depravation of Judeo-Christian messianism. Needless to say, that is the reason why it can be an urgent spiritual temptation today for European intellectuals. (Gnosticism is no danger for Americans, always essentially practical and seldom really tempted by messianism, Christian or otherwise.)

In any case the Christian contemplative today should be acquainted with the broad outline of the dialectical mystique. For the Christian too has a mystique of history. He too is committed by his faith to a contemplative view of man, in which history is oriented to a final discovery and revelation of Man in God and God in Man at the Parousia. And a rediscovery of the inner meaning of the New Testament may perhaps startle him with the realization that this revelation of the Mystery of God and Man in Christ, the Mystical Body, is not something we can passively anticipate. It is something that we are called to *bring about by the action of our creative freedom.* The Russian Orthodox existentialist Nicholas Berdyaev[10] has emphasized this truth more clearly and urgently than any other modern thinker. This is one of the great, neglected Christian discoveries of our time. He says:

> It is particularly important to rise above the passive interpretation of the Apocalypse as the expectation of the end and of the Last Judgment. It is possible to interpret it actively as a call to creative activity, to heroic effort and achievement. The end depends to a certain extent on man and the nature of it will be determined by man's activity. (*The Destiny of Man*, p. 290)

Obviously, this must be understood in a Christian sense. Man's activity according to Berdyaev is not the Promethean struggle to divinize himself by technics and power, but the free cooperation of his creative love with the love of God, which will lead him to fulfill his true vocation to divinity as a son of God.

It is precisely because the Christian view of history has lost too many of its contemplative and mystical elements that it has become something inert and passive, a mere reactionary obscurantism that tolerates injustice and abuse on earth for the sake of a compensation in the afterlife. Marxism pours scorn on this kind of religion and takes advantage of its deficiencies to caricature it without mercy. In this way, the Marxist is able to steal from Christianity one of its most potent and characteristic claims: that it has come to divinize the freedom and the spirit of man. Christians, hearing this for the first time, forgetting that their baptism is a new birth as children of God with a vocation to the highest creative responsibilities, have not understood the hidden implication of this claim made blasphemous only by its separation from its true context. In reality, the Marxists have insolently taken upon themselves, in their own way, the task that was given to us by Christ the Lord of History and which we have failed to accept from His hand. It is once again the story of those who were invited to the wedding feast and did not come. And now the parable applies not to the Jews, but to ourselves . . .

All this is to say that Christian contemplation cannot consist merely in a dark withdrawal into subjective peace, without reference to the rest of the world. A contemplation that merely hides in subjectivity and individualism is a by-product of the bourgeois spirituality we have discussed above. It is a comfortable negation of the present life, which is not really a negation of anything, but only an evasion of responsibility in order to enjoy interior comfort. Quietism is a bourgeois phenomenon, and is the spiritual counterpart to the individualistic love of material comfort together with the intellectual and spiritual laziness characteristic of the middle class.

It would be wrong to react against this with sheer activism. That is the danger of the more extreme endeavors that have attempted to integrate Christianity into working-class movements. They have allowed themselves to be carried away by political delusions and have put more trust in the words and tactics of pressure groups than in the Spirit of God. But this is precisely the age-old temptation of the People of God, the idolatry that was lashed out at by Moses and the Prophets, the hardness of heart that called forth Christ's tears over Jerusalem.

Is there, indeed, a mysterious stream of reality and of meaning running through the history of mankind? If so, who is called to discover it and travel with it? Such a mystery is mere symbol, and if we take it too seriously, too literally, we will be deceived by our own symbolism. The inner reality of man's history is man himself, man the son and the image of God. This reality is not only human but divine, for God has united man to Himself in Christ. But this divine reality, which is the heart of history, though it can be conceptualized and symbolized, can never be fully grasped or contained in a symbol. One may isolate the reality in a symbol, but then one must remember that it is not the symbol, and that the symbol itself is incapable of communicating the full reality. So that one must be able to say, immediately after using the symbol, "But the reality is not that." What is the reality? The only answer is that it is Unknown, but that one knows it by unknowing.

Such a reality as this is bound to be a fatal stumbling block for politicians. The politician, the technocrat, the engineer of society, the practical man, is the one who is congenitally incapable of grasping it. For he always sees it as an object, as a "thing," as a "force," as something that can be measured and brought into line. But as soon as you start to measure it, it is no longer there. As soon as you start to plan with it or for it, it has evaded you. In reality, those who try to control and use history are controlled and used by it: which is to say, they are controlled and used by one another. They are the creatures of their own machinery, the prisoners of their own past and their own future.

This brings us again to the necessity for a deep contemplative penetration of reality. The phrase is misleading in itself, of course. But anyone who has carefully followed the treatment of the subject in the pages of this book will by now instinctively make the right adjustment. The "reality" through which the contemplative "penetrates" in order to reach a contact with what is "ultimate" in it is actually his own being, his own life. The contemplative is not one who directs a magic spiritual intuition upon other objects, but one who, being perfectly unified in himself and recollected in the center of his own humility, enters into contact with reality by an immediacy that forgets the division between subject and object. In a certain sense, by losing himself and by forgetting himself as an object of reflection, he finds himself and all other reality together. This "finding" is beyond concepts and beyond practical projects.

The contemplative does not set out to achieve a kind of intuitive mastery of history, or of man's spirit, or of the things of God. He seeks the center of his own living truth, and there all that he needs to perceive of these other mysteries is granted to him at the moment when he needs it. If he needs nothing, nothing is granted. And if nothing is granted, nothing is desired. The wisdom of the contemplative is, then, not the wisdom of a man who needs to possess knowledge and learning (though he may be a learned man). It is the wisdom of a man who has forgotten himself and forgotten wisdom, and who seeks to possess nothing because he needs nothing. All that he needs comes to him from God, even before he begins to need it.

It may at first sight seem absurd to think that the development of man's society could owe anything to such a detached and disinterested being as this. This is perhaps because we have accepted the noisy delusions of the politician with too much confidence. Yet the helplessness and passivity of the politician are beginning to be quite evident, in spite of all his noise and bluster. It is clear that though he thinks he is leading, he is being led. Though he thinks he is acting, he is acted upon. And when we consider *what*[11] weapons he has in his hand, this realization is singularly disquieting.

To praise the contemplative life is not to reject every other form of life, but to seek a solid foundation for every other human striving. Without the silence and recollection of the interior life, man loses contact with his real sources of energy, clarity, and peace. When he tries to be his own god and insists on keeping his hands on everything, remembering everything and controlling everything, he drives himself to ruin. For when man thinks himself powerful, then at every moment he is in desperate need: he is in need of knowledge, strength, control, and he depends on countless instruments. But when man remembers the unfailing power of God and realizes that because he is the son of God, this power *already belongs to him*, then he does not have to think anymore about the things he needs. For what he needs will be given him when he needs it, and in this sense, God will think and act for him.

Modern man may have been tempted to look upon this as an evasion. In actual fact it is the highest and simplest courage: the courage without which life cannot be faced as it is and loses its real meaning. This was the central message of the Sermon on the Mount:

> Be not solicitous for your life, what you shall eat, nor for your body, what you shall put on. Is not the life more than the meat, and the body more than the raiment? Behold the birds of the air, for they neither sow, nor do they reap, nor gather into barns: and your heavenly Father feedeth them. Are not you of much more value than they? . . . Be not therefore solicitous for the morrow: for the morrow will be solicitous for itself. Sufficient for the day is the evil thereof. (Matthew 6)

It is fashionable today to point to the evil in the world as though it could be put forward as evidence against this teaching on Providence. But the ironical thing is that the greatest evils in the world today (wars, genocide, slave labor, mass exile, poverty, and degradation) are all the direct result of man's rejection of this teaching of Christ. We cannot serve two masters. If we have rejected God and chosen Mammon, and if the result is what we were told to expect, then why do we complain?

The contemplative life is, then, a matter of the greatest importance for modern man and is important to him in all that is most valuable in his ideal. Today more than ever, man in chains is seeking emancipation and liberty. His tragedy is *that he seeks*[12] it by means that bring him into ever greater enslavement. But freedom is a spiritual thing. It is a sacred and religious reality. Its roots are not in man, but in God. For man's freedom, which makes him the image of God, is a participation in the freedom of God. Man is free insofar as he is like God. His struggle for freedom means, then, a struggle to renounce a false, illusory autonomy in order to become free beyond and above himself. In other words, for man to be free he must be delivered *from himself*. This means not that he must be delivered only from another like himself: for the tyranny of man over man is but the external expression of each man's enslavement to his own desires. For he who is the slave of his own desires necessarily exploits others in order to pay tribute to the tyrant within himself.

Before there can be any external freedom, man must learn to find the way to freedom within himself. For only then can he afford to relax his grip on others, and let them get away from him, because then he does not need their dependence. It is the contemplative who keeps this liberty alive in the world, and who shows others, obscurely and without realizing it, what real freedom means.

That was why St. Gregory of Nyssa said that the contemplative, who had restored in his own soul the image of God, was the truly free man: for he alone could walk with God as Adam had walked with Him in Paradise. He alone could stand and speak freely to God his Father, with complete confidence. He alone could worthily bear his dignity as son of God and king of God's creation:

> The human soul then manifests its proud royal character, far from all baseness, in that it is without master, autonomous, disposing of itself sovereignly by its own decisions. Indeed is not our soul the image of Him Who reigns over all? It is precisely in this royal dignity, in which it was created, that resides the soul's likeness to God. (*De Hominis Opificio, Patrologia Graeca*, 44, 136)

[APPENDIX A]

References to 'The Inner Experience'

In the Merton Journals

July 12, 1959: "This week I have been rewriting 'What Is Contemplation?' and of course it has come out about three times as long and is a completely different book. A lot of water has gone under the bridge since 1948 [the year when *What Is Contemplation?* was written]. How poor were all my oversimplified ideas—and how mistaken I was to make contemplation only *part* of a man's life. For a contemplative his whole life is contemplation The last part of the book is turning into a vocal protest against *vanitas monastica* [monastic pride]. I protest too much. It is a sign of weakness and bad conscience. I will have to revise all that" (vol. 3, *A Search for Solitude,* ed. Lawrence S. Cunningham [San Francisco: Harper San Francisco, 1996], 303).

July 21, 1959: "Rewriting *What Is Contemplation?*—making too many cracks about 'large monasteries' which are 'like factories'" (*Search for Solitude,* 308).

August 9, 1959: "The second ¹/₂ of the transformed version of *What Is Contemplation?* (totally reformed) seems satisfactory. The 1st., in which much of the old is left, is poor" (*Search for Solitude,* 316).

September 6, 1959: "Some rewriting on *Inner Experience* which is now, I think, a respectable book" (*Search for Solitude,* 327).

September 29, 1959: "My last mss. ('The Inner Experience') lies on the desk untouched. I want to revise it. I want to clean up that room. And get rid of a lot of things and clear the decks for action" (*Search for Solitude,* 332).

November 19, 1959: "*Three books* to finish correcting and proofreading and that's all— the future, if it wants another, will have to say how six or seven years from now."

A   The Essays—and Xstian Life of Prayer
B   Existential Communion
C   Inner Experience (?)
(*Search for Solitude,* 346)

August 26, 1963: "Tried to get some of my unfinished work together. With revision of several essays, etc. And revision of *The Inner Experience.* I have still four or five books on hand, not counting *Prayer as Worship [and Experience],* etc." (vol. 5, *Dancing in the Water of Life,* ed. Robert E. Daggy [San Francisco: Harper San Francisco, 1997], 13).

In the Merton Letters

TO SISTER THÉRÈSE LENTFOEHR

July 4, 1959: "At the moment, guess what, I am rewriting *What Is Contemplation.* It will be a patchy job. But I have been wanting to do it. I may revise other early material, too. It is all very unsatisfactory to me, in fact a lot of it disgusts me. I was much too superficial and too cerebral at the same time. I seem to have ignored the wholeness and integrity of life, and concentrated on a kind of angelism in contemplation. That was when I was a rip-roaring Trappist, I guess. Now that I am a little less perfect, I seem to have a saner perspective. And that too seems to be not according to the manuals, doesn't it?" (vol. 2, *The Road to Joy,* ed. Robert E. Daggy [New York: Farrar, Straus and Giroux, 1989], 233).

September 29, 1959: "I finished a book this summer called *The Inner Experience* which started out to be a simple revision of *What Is Contemplation* but turned into something new, and just about full length. It has to be revised and has been sitting here on the desk, waiting for revision for some time, but I refuse to work around the house as they are blasting around on all sides with jackhammers and other machines and it is impossible to think. The novices have been making a good share of this noise, trying to put in a couple of new showers in our crowded cellar" (*Road to Joy,* 233–34).

TO CZESLAW MILOSZ

September 12, 1959: "I have just been finishing another book, *The Inner Experience*—a wider deeper view of the same thing, contemplation, with more reference to Oriental ideas. There is to me nothing but this that counts, but everything can enter into it" (vol. 4, *The Courage for Truth,* ed. Christine M. Bochen [New York: Farrar, Straus and Giroux, 1993], 63).

Tables of Contents: A Comparison

		PAGES	
CHAPTERS	Draft 2	Draft 4	Published Text
I. A Preliminary Warning	1–5	1–5	1–5
II. The Awakening of the Inner Self	6–16	6–16	6–18
III. Society and the Inner Self	17–33	17–33	19–34
IV. Christian Contemplation	34–54	34–54	35–56
V.[1] Kinds of Contemplation	55–56[2]	55–69	57–70
VI.[3] Infused Contemplation	missing	70–77b[4] (added)	71–79
VII.[5] Five Texts on Contemplative Prayer	7 pages (no numbers)	78–84	80–88
VIII. The Paradox of the Illuminative Way	5 pages (no numbers)	85–89	89–94
IX.[6] What to Do: The Teaching of St. John of the Cross	missing	90–94 (added)	95–100
X.[7] Some Dangers	53–61	95–103	101–109
XI. Contemplation and Neurosis	62–66	104–108	110–114
XII. The Desire of Contemplation	67–69	109–111	115–117
XIII. The Sense of Sin	70–74	112–116	118–122
XIV. Problems of the Contemplative Life	75–95	117–137	123–141
XV. Prospects and Conclusions	99–108	138–150	142–154

Notes

Introduction

1. *A Search for Solitude: Pursuing the Monk's True Life,* vol. 3 of *The Journals of Thomas Merton,* ed. Lawrence S. Cunningham (San Francisco: Harper San Francisco, 1996), 303.
2. *The Road to Joy: The Letters of Thomas Merton to Old and New Friends,* vol. 2 of *The Letters of Thomas Merton,* ed. Robert E. Daggy (New York: Farrar, Straus and Giroux, 1989), 233.
3. *Search for Solitude,* 308. See Chapter 14, p. 125, 131.
4. *Search for Solitude,* 327.
5. *The Courage for Truth: The Letters of Thomas Merton to Writers,* vol. 4 of *The Letters of Thomas Merton,* ed. Christine M. Bochen (New York: Farrar, Straus and Giroux, 1993), 63.
6. *Road to Joy,* 233–34.
7. *Search for Solitude,* 332.
8. *Search for Solitude,* 346.
9. *Dancing in the Water of Life: Seeking Peace in the Hermitage,* vol. 5 of *The Journals of Thomas Merton,* ed. Robert E. Daggy (San Francisco: Harper San Francisco, 1997), 13.
10. Merton Legacy Trust, archives, Thomas Merton Center, Louisville, Kentucky.
11. John Slate died September 19, 1967. Hence he was not able to serve as a member of the Trust.
12. *Road to Joy,* 301.
13. Walsh had no idea of the time of the writing of "The Inner Experience." He writes to Father Flavian: "Tom seems to have tried in this work to bring together and follow up on his previous work in *The New Man, New Seeds of Contemplation* and *Zen and the Birds of Appetite.*" This is clearly incorrect. It is not consistent with Merton's words to Walsh that this was "something I wrote a long time ago." It also conflicts with the references in both the *Letters* and the *Journals* that definitely indicate that that "a long time ago" was the summer of 1959.
14. This was published by Farrar, Straus and Giroux. A considerably revised version of this work, with more reflection on the "inner experience," was published by St. Anthony Messenger Press in 2000 with a new title, *Thomas Merton's Paradise Journey.*

15. New York: Paulist Press.

16. The numbering of the four drafts comes not from Merton, but from the curator of the Thomas Merton Center (possibly Dr. Robert E. Daggy). The original typescript that Merton gave to Daniel Walsh has no draft designation (though it clearly is the same text as what I have called draft 4).

17. It is worth noting that Merton's original title for this work was *The Dark Path*. This is on the title page of draft 1 but is crossed out and has *The Inner Experience* written over it. The title *The Dark Path* occurs later in draft 1, at the beginning of the insertions.

18. I have stressed this 1959 date for the writing of *The Inner Experience* because others have consistently placed it later. Raymond Bailey, in his book *Thomas Merton on Mysticism* (New York: Doubleday, 1975), cites Brother Patrick Hart as saying that the first draft of *The Inner Experience* was written in 1961. Brother Patrick has told me that this is incorrect. Michael Casey, in his 1993 article on *The Inner Experience* in the Australian publication *Tjurunga*, writes: "From 1961 he produced no less than four drafts." Anne E. Carr, in *A Search for Wisdom: Thomas Merton's Theology of the Self* (Notre Dame, IN: University of Notre Dame Press, 1988), states that Merton finished the fourth draft shortly before he left for Asia in 1968 (p. 153). This is correct, but misleading. It would be clearer to say that in 1968 he made minor corrections and additions to a 1959 text.

19. *Seeds of Contemplation* (New York: New Directions, 1949), 28: "Every one of us is shadowed by an illusory person: a false self."

20. See *Disputed Questions* (New York: Farrar, Straus and Cudahy, 1960), 206–207.

21. In 1959 he was reading D.T. Suzuki's *Essays in Zen Buddhism* and quotes from the second of the series of three books published under that title.

22. See p. 87, where Merton speaks of "the sensual dreams of the Sufis." This statement was omitted in the (slightly) revised edition of December 1949.

23. See especially Chapter 10.

24. See, e.g., Chapter 14, pp. 137–38.

25. I would venture the opinion that most commentators have read only abbreviated versions of *The Inner Experience* and not the unabridged version, which up to now has been available only in duplicated form at the Thomas Merton Center at Bellarmine University.

26. Michael Casey, "Merton's Notes on 'Inner Experience' Twenty-five Years Afterwards," *Tjurunga* 44 (1993): 32.

Chapter One: A Preliminary Warning

1. "sometimes": insert. (Note: All inserts or substitutions are handwritten and were incorporated into the text in 1968. See Introduction.)
2. "important" replaces "essential."
3. "it fits in with your plans" replaces "you like it."
4. "punish" replaces "insult."
5. "deliver" replaces "have."
6. "The Eastern traditions . . . for contemplation": insert.
7. "reintegrate" replaces "dissolve."
8. "human person" replaces "personal being."

9. "subject": insert.

10. "an object" replaces "a being." By 1968 Merton had long been occupied with the relation of "subject" and "object."

11. "his experience of himself is an experience of God" replaces "this is contemplation."

12. "peaceful" replaces "safe."

Chapter Two: The Awakening of the Inner Self

1. "existential": insert.

2. "his" replaces "its."

3. "Nevertheless a certain cultural . . . educated and enlightened minority": insert.

4. "Zen is, in a sense, antimystical": insert.

5. These lines enclosed in brackets are crossed out by a single stroke that does not hide them. There are four such groups of lines in this chapter, and all of them are about Eastern thought. Assuming these lines were written in 1959 (a valid assumption since these lines are found on draft 2, which was certainly written in 1959), one may wonder whether Merton may have had some misgivings about including them. He was just becoming comfortable with Eastern language about what he saw as a mystical strain in Buddhism.

6. See note 5 above.

7. The Sung dynasty ruled China from 960 to 1269.

8. "Yet these are . . . self and not-self": insert.

9. "or 'suchness'": insert.

10. This poem may be found in D. T. Suzuki, *Essays in Zen Buddhism, Second Series* (1953; reprint, London: Rider, 1970), 37.

11. Here are Suzuki's words: "How barren, how unromantic *satori* is when compared with the Christian mystic experiences!" (*Essays in Zen Buddhism, Second Series*, 38).

12. "this experience" replaces "it."

13. "affective or": insert.

14. "no familiar name" replaces three completely blocked-out words.

15. "beyond yes and no, subject and object, self and not-self" replaces a heavily crossed-out section of three lines.

16. "like": insert.

17. "Christian" replaces "man."

18. See note 5 above.

19. "awareness of": insert.

20. "inner" replaces "placid."

21. See note 5 above.

22. John Tauler (ca. 1300–1361) was a German Dominican and mystical writer, a disciple of Meister Eckhart.

23. Meister Eckhart (ca. 1260–ca. 1328) was a Dominican theologian and spiritual writer. His writings on the relation of God and creatures were seen by some of his contemporaries as blurring the distinction between God and humans. Some of his statements were condemned as heretical, though his defenders say that such a judgment is based on a mistaken understanding of what he wrote and said.

24. "effective" replaces "good."

25. St. John of the Cross (1542–91), a Doctor of the Church and a reformer (with the help of St. Teresa of Avila) of the Carmelite Order, was one of the great Spanish poets and mystics. His four major writings are *The Ascent of Mount Carmel, The Dark Night of the Soul, The Spiritual Canticle,* and *The Living Flame of Love.* The mystical poems he wrote are most important in understanding his spirituality.

Chapter Three: Society and the Inner Self

1. "isolation and": insert.

2. "All the more . . . personal 'subjects'": insert.

3. Philoxenus of Mabbugh (ca. 450–523), born in Tahal, Persia, was a Syrian bishop and influential Monophysite theologian. An original thinker inspired by the Alexandrian school of theology, he strongly opposed the Council of Chalcedon. He is honored by the Jacobite (Monophysite) Church as a saint and Doctor of the Church. Some eighty works of his survive, including five tracts on the Incarnation and the Trinity.

4. "exaggeration of" replaces two blotted-out and unreadable words.

5. "discover" replaces "find."

6. "interest or": insert.

7. "unconscious" replaces "somehow subconscious."

8. "or a consummation": insert.

9. "Reins" is an archaic form in earlier versions of the Bible. Literally it means kidneys; figuratively, the seat of feelings or affections.

10. "psychic": insert.

11. "painful or happy": insert.

12. "fruits of the earth" replaces "vegetation."

13. "political idols" replaces a deleted and illegible word.

14. "seem to": insert.

15. Søren Kierkegaard (1813–55) was a Danish religious philosopher whose writings prepared the way for existentialism. In *Fear and Trembling,* he discusses the meaning of faith and sees in Abraham and his willingness to sacrifice his own son at God's command a model of true faith, namely, absolute obedience to the Absolute.

16. "Note the analogies . . . concept of *karma*": insert.

17. The *Bhagavad Gita* is a sacred Hindu text that forms part of the larger Sanskrit epic *The Mahabharata.* The *Gita* takes the form of a philosophical dialogue between Lord Krishna and the warrior-prince Arjuna on ethical issues and on the nature of God. The dialogue takes place on a field of battle.

18. "This omission is no longer pardonable": deleted.

19. In *What Is Contemplation?* Merton had used the term "quasi-contemplatives" (see, e.g., *What Is Contemplation?* [Springfield, IL: Templegate Publishers, 1981], 32) to describe what he called "active contemplatives." Jacques Maritain had suggested to him that "masked contemplatives" might be a better term. Merton adopted his suggestion. In his letter to Maritain in *The Courage for Truth,* he says: "Thank you for your kind remarks on *What Is Contemplation?,* and I especially like the term 'masked contemplatives,' which expresses much better what I mean" (p. 24).

20. Reginald Garrigou-Lagrange (1877–1964) was a French Dominican theologian and writer on spirituality. From 1909 to 1960 he taught fundamental, dogmatic, and spiritual theology

at the Angelicum (the University of St. Thomas Aquinas) in Rome. He published many books in theology and spirituality and served as consultor to the Holy See.

21. See Merton's *The Wisdom of the Desert.*

Chapter Four: Christian Contemplation

1. This is Merton's paraphrase of John 17:3.

2. St. Athanasius (d. 373) was a strong defender of the Council of Nicaea against Arius, who denied the divinity of Christ. His notable writings include *On the Incarnation* and *Discourses Against the Arians.*

3. "borrowed from St. Irenaeus": insert. St. Irenaeus (ca. 130–ca. 200), a native of Smyrna, became bishop of Lyons. He was the first theologian to offer a comprehensive account of Christian belief. His most famous work, *Adversus Haereses (Against Heresies),* is an anti-Gnostic treatise in five books. Against the Gnostics, he argued that there is no sacred teaching apart from the rule of faith handed down and guaranteed by the apostolic succession of the bishops. Against the Gnostic teaching on the evil of material reality, he taught that Christ "recapitulated" in himself God's designs for humanity.

4. "one": insert.

5. St. Maximus the Confessor (ca. 580–662) was a Byzantine theologian who defended and developed the teaching of the Council of Chalcedon. His teaching on the humanity and divinity of Christ was especially honored in monastic circles in the East.

6. "focused" replaces "centered."

7. This is the first portion of *What Is Contemplation?* that appears in *The Inner Experience.* Everything from *What Is Contemplation?* is in this different type font and the page references are to the Templegate edition of *What Is Contemplation?* (Springfield, IL: Templegate Publishers, 1981). Hereafter Templegate. This quotation appears on p. 13.

8. Translation: "Gift of God most high."

9. Templegate, 13–14.

10. This thought is developed in *Seeds of Contemplation* (1949).

11. Templegate, 14–17.

12. Templegate, 17–18. Following the quotation from 1 Corinthians, *What Is Contemplation?* introduces as a heading before the next section: "St. Thomas Aquinas." This is not included in any of the drafts of *The Inner Experience.*

13. Templegate, 19.

14. "superficial" replaces "temporal." This may have been done in the 1959 revision.

15. Translation: "Spiritual things cannot be seen, unless one is emptied of worldly things."

16. "trivial" replaces a word that is blotted out.

17. Translation: "Spiritual gifts are not received unless they are desired."

18. Translation: "They are not desired unless they are known in some way."

19. "alienated" replaces "worldly."

20. Translation: "Taste and see that the Lord is sweet."

21. Templegate, 19–23.

22. Blaise Pascal (1623–62) was a French mathematician and religious thinker. Through his contact with Port Royal, he became involved in the rigorism of the Jansenist movement. His most enduring legacy is the classic *Pensées,* his defense of Christianity against unbelievers.

23. "learn" replaces "come."
24. Templegate, 23–24.

Chapter Five: Kinds of Contemplation

1. In the final draft (1968) this chapter is labeled Chapter 4, as was the previous chapter. Clearly it should be Chapter 5.
2. "represent" replaces three blotted-out words.
3. "effected" replaces two blotted-out words.
4. "from" replaces "out of."
5. Hebrews 4:12.
6. "Certain" replaces "The."
7. "awareness" replaces "experience."
8. "inmost": insert.
9. "Baptism sanctifies us . . . 'new man in Christ' ": insert.
10. "one" replaces "he."
11. "entirely" replaces "wholely."
12. "extremely simple" replaces "humble," the word used in *What Is Contemplation?*
13. "hidden contemplatives" in *The Inner Experience* replaces "quasi-contemplatives" in *What Is Contemplation?*
14. Jacques Maritain, after reading *What Is Contemplation?*, suggested the term "masked contemplatives" instead of "quasi-contemplatives." Merton accepted his suggestion. See Merton's letter to Maritain of February 10, 1949, in *The Courage for Truth: Letters of Thomas Merton to Writers*, ed. Christine M. Bochen (New York: Farrar, Straus and Giroux, 1993), 24.
15. *What Is Contemplation?* (Springfield, IL: Templegate Publishers, 1981), 30–35.
16. Pseudo-Dionysius (also known as Denys the Areopagite or simply Dionysius) was a pseudonymous writer of the fifth or early sixth century who wrote in Greek. His works exerted a major influence on the development of Western spirituality. He is primarily associated with apophatic theology (the way of negation and darkness); see, for example, his *Mystical Theology*, though he also wrote about the kataphatic way (see especially *The Divine Names* and *The Celestial Hierarchy*).
17. St. Anthony of Egypt (ca. 251–356), the prototype of the monks of the desert, retired in early adulthood into the Egyptian desert for a life of solitude, penance, prayer, and work. He is best known through a hagiographical story of his life written by St. Athanasius.
18. "temporal": insert.
19. "down" replaces "across."
20. "fruitlessly" replaces "uselessly."
21. "passive": insert.
22. "exterior": insert.
23. "He has to": insert.
24. "is completed in mystical intuition": insert.
25. "our inmost": insert.
26. "inner": insert.
27. St. Gregory of Nyssa (ca. 335–95), bishop and theologian, was the younger brother of St. Basil the Great. Of special interest is his *Life of Moses*—a work in the apophatic tradition—

which sees Moses' ascent of Mount Sinai as a mystical experience of never ending enjoyment of God.

28. "natural" replaces "created."
29. "This is infused . . . sense of the term": insert.

Chapter Six: Infused Contemplation

1. This chapter is listed as 7. Clearly it should be 6.
2. "toward" replaces "to be."
3. Translation: "Divine reality is experienced."
4. "It is beyond feeling, even beyond concepts": insert.
5. "(intuitive)": insert.
6. "final ecstatic": insert.
7. In *What Is Contemplation?* this text is preceded by the title "Infused Contemplation," the same as the title of this chapter of *The Inner Experience.*
8. Translation: "He first loved us."
9. In *What Is Contemplation?* this section has the title "St. Bernard of Clairvaux."

   St. Bernard (1090–1153) was a Cistercian abbot and spiritual writer. At the age of twenty-one he entered the new, struggling community at Cîteaux, persuading some thirty of his relatives and friends to join him. Three years later he was sent out to found the monastery at Clairvaux. His writings (e.g., his eighty-six sermons on the Canticle of Canticles; his masterpiece, *On the Love of God;* and his *De Consideratione*) were a formative influence on Cistercian spirituality. He preached the Second Crusade, which proved a disaster and a humiliation to him. His long work, *De Consideratione,* was written at the request of Pope Eugenius III, who had been a monk of Clairvaux.
10. Translation: "Love needs no cause except itself nor fruit save itself: its fruit is its use."
11. *What Is Contemplation?* (Springfield, IL: Templegate Publishers, 1981), 36–40. Hereafter Templegate.
12. "depths" replaces "heights."
13. "surround" replaces "come to."
14. "sphere" replaces "depth."
15. "As Eckhart says . . . no questions": insert.
16. "weakened by its own": insert.
17. "rejects" replaces "denies."
18. "carries out" replaces "launches."
19. Templegate, 41–46.
20. Note the use here and in the closing paragraphs of the chapter of the older term "Holy Ghost" instead of "Holy Spirit."
21. "sanely traditional": insert.
22. "society" replaces "institution."
23. "society" replaces "institution."
24. "spiritual": insert.
25. "contumacy" replaces "disobedience."
26. "intractable willfulness" replaces "self-will."
27. "man" replaces "monk."

28. "aspirations" replaces "attractions."
29. "and follow him": deleted.

Chapter Seven: Five Texts on Contemplative Prayer

1. The text that makes up this chapter has no chapter number in the draft. It may serve as an appendix to the previous chapter, or its last part may be preparation for the next chapter, on the illuminative way. Hence it seems appropriate to give it its own proper chapter number (7).
2. Blessed John van Ruysbroeck (1293–1381) was a fourteenth-century Flemish mystic. An Augustinian canon, at an early age he retired to a hermitage at Groenendaal (near Brussels), where he became prior of a small community. Noted for his sanctity, he had many coming to him for counsel. Among his disciples were John Tauler and Gerard Groote.
3. *The Cloud of Unknowing* is an anonymous work on the mystical life written in England in the fourteenth century. The author, who may have been a Carthusian, draws on the apophatic tradition of Pseudo-Dionysius. The *Cloud* expresses the need to withdraw by putting all created things under a cloud of forgetfulness in order to pierce the cloud of unknowing and come to experience God by love.
4. "it is our inmost self": insert.
5. "ordinary" replaces "natural."
6. "secular" replaces "worldly."
7. In *What Is Contemplation?* the corresponding section begins: "Finally, the surest sign of infused contemplation beyond the cloud of darkness is a powerful, mysterious and yet simple attraction which holds the soul prisoner in this darkness and obscurity."
8. "noonday" replaces "the brightest day."
9. Translation: "Love draws all else to itself and captivates the affections."
10. At this point *What Is Contemplation?* has "becomes adorned with many virtues." Merton changed it to "free, virtuous, and strong." Presumably this change was made in 1959, as it is already in the text and not a 1968 insert.
11. *What Is Contemplation?* (Springfield, IL: Templegate Publishers, 1981), 51–54. The Templegate text adds to the end of the final sentence: "in which sanctity and true contemplation are found."

Chapter Eight: The Paradox of the Illuminative Way

1. Merton seems to set this material up as a separate section, though he does not give it a chapter number. I have chosen to treat it as a separate chapter, though it could well be linked to the preceding chapter, which is also without a chapter number.
2. "inmost": insert.

Chapter Nine: What to Do: The Teaching of St. John of the Cross

1. In *What Is Contemplation?* Merton had included this description of St. John of the Cross: "one of the greatest as well as the safest mystical theologians God has given to His Church."

2. Merton does indeed label this section Chapter 9. This suggests he may well have thought of the two previous sections as separate chapters. Note: Most of the material in this chapter and its title are taken directly from *What Is Contemplation?*

3. In the 1959 draft "reality" replaces "object," the word used in *What Is Contemplation?*

4. Same as the preceding note.

5. *What Is Contemplation?* (Springfield, IL: Templegate Publishers, 1981), 55–65.

6. "and crosses" found in *What Is Contemplation?* but omitted in *The Inner Experience.*

7. Templegate, 65–67.

Chapter Ten: Some Dangers

1. It was Merton himself who labeled this Chapter 10, which seems to justify the labeling I have given to the previous unnumbered chapters. In *What Is Contemplation?* this chapter is called "The Danger of Quietism."

2. "face with faith and abandonment" replaces "overcome by love and faith and Christian virtue" (*What Is Contemplation?* [Springfield, IL: Templegate Publishers, 1981], 72).

3. *What Is Contemplation?* Templegate, 68–78. Except for one additional paragraph and a prayer to the "Father and Maker of Love," *What Is Contemplation?* ends at this point. This prayer to the Father is in the Templegate edition of 1981, which used the text of the British edition published in 1950 by Burns Oates in London. This edition was part of a series called the Pater Noster books, hence the appropriateness of the prayer to the Father. The St. Mary's edition, published in 1948, concludes, appropriately, with a prayer to Mary: "Immaculate Heart of the Virgin Mother of God . . . "

4. "nonreligious": insert.

5. Paul Tillich (1886–1965) was a German Protestant theologian who influenced both Protestant and Catholic thinkers in the United States and in Europe. Among his many writings may be mentioned *Shaking the Foundations, The Courage to Be,* and *Dynamics of Faith.*

6. Jean-Paul Sartre (1905–80) was a French existentialist philosopher, playwright, and novelist. Influenced by the writings of Heidegger, he saw humans as lonely beings carrying the burden of a terrifying freedom to choose and yet finding themselves adrift in a world of meaninglessness. His writings include *Nausea, No Exit, Being and Nothingness,* and *The Age of Reason,* as well as his autobiography, *The Words.*

7. French philosopher Gabriel Marcel (1889–1973) saw philosophy as a reflection on human experience. His writings include *The Philosophy of Existentialism, The Mystery of Being,* and *Being and Having.*

8. Nicholas Berdyaev (1874–1948) was a Russian Orthodox religious thinker whose philosophy of personalism, freedom, and creativity links him spiritually with the West, though elements of the Russian worldview of such writers as Dostoyevsky made their impression on his thought. Among his writings may be listed *The Philosophy of Freedom, The Meaning of Creativity,* and *Destiny of Man.*

9. The French Thomist philosopher Jacques Maritain (1882–1973) taught at the Institut Catholique in Paris, then later at the Medieval Institute in Toronto and at Princeton University. He served as French ambassador to the Vatican from 1945 to 1948. In 1970 he joined the congregation of the Little Brothers of Jesus. His writings include *The Degrees of*

Knowledge and *Creative Intuition in Art and Poetry.* His disappointment with the Second Vatican Council finds expression in his *The Peasant of the Garonne.*

10. Boris Leonidovich Pasternak (1890–1960), Russian poet and translator, became the world symbol of the artist in conflict with the political environment. This was especially true of his book *Doctor Zhivago.* The book won him a Nobel prize, which he had to refuse because of political pressures. Merton was very much attracted to Pasternak and wrote to him and about him (see *Pasternak-Merton: Six Letters, The Courage for Truth,* and essays in *Disputed Questions*).

11. "spiritual": insert.

12. Ronald Arbuthnott Knox (1888–1957), an Anglican who became a Roman Catholic in 1917, was ordained a priest in 1919, became chaplain of the Catholic students at Oxford, and translated the Latin Vulgate Bible into English. Notable among his writings are *A Spiritual Aeneid* and *Enthusiasm,* a history of charismatic, sectarian movements in Christianity.

13. Aldous Huxley (1894–1963) was an English novelist who in his later works showed an interest in mysticism, Eastern and Western. His *Ends and Means* (on mysticism) was an important influence on Merton during his Columbia years.

14. "falsification" replaces "falsity."

15. "mystical" replaces "spiritual."

16. "medically": insert.

Chapter Eleven: Contemplation and Neurosis

1. "sets out to conquer this realm" replaces "embarks on a life."

2. "Evidently" replaces "Obviously."

Chapter Twelve: The Desire of Contemplation

1. "experiential awareness" replaces "experience."

2. The American philosopher William James (1842–1910) was a pragmatist who wrote of a philosophy of direct experience. His works include *The Principles of Psychology* (1890) and *The Varieties of Religious Experience* (1902).

3. "inescapable" replaces an unreadable, blotted-out word.

4. "communion" replaces "contact."

Chapter Thirteen: The Sense of Sin

1. "think" replaces "believe."

2. In *No Exit* three persons find themselves in a room from which they can never emerge and in which they can never get along with one another. Near the end of the play one of the characters, Garcin, declares: "So this is hell. I'd never have believed it. You remember all we were told about the torture-chambers, the fire and brimstone, the 'burning marl.' Old wives' tales! There is no need for red-hot pokers. Hell is—other people!" ("No Exit," in *Twenty Best European Plays on the American Stage,* ed. John Gassner [New York: Crown, 1959], 299).

3. "part of": insert.

4. "Jeremias" is the spelling used in the Latin Vulgate and the Douai-Rheims Bible for "Jeremiah."

5. "mean" replaces "be."

6. A city of southern Poland, west of Cracow, Auschwitz was the site of the largest Nazi concentration and extermination camp during World War II; it is now called Oswiecim.

7. Dachau, a German city northwest of Munich, was the site of another Nazi concentration and extermination camp; it was built in 1935 and liberated by the Allies in 1945.

8. Located in the White Sea near the Polar Circle (Russia) is the Solovetski (Solovky) archipelago. The largest island, Solovky, once housed a monastery. Since the sixteenth century it has served as a prison. Beginning in the 1920s, one of the first Soviet labor camps was located on Solovky. The labor camp existed there till 1939, during which time hundreds of thousands of political prisoners were tortured and killed there. Alexander Solzhenitsyn's novel *One Day in the Life of Ivan Denisovich* takes place in Solovky camp. In 1990 the monastery was founded again, and about thirty monks live there.

9. Karaganda is located on the arid steppe of northern Kazakhstan. In the early 1930s it was the site of one of the largest Soviet labor camps.

10. Literally, "twilight of the gods." The term can be used to designate the turbulent ending of a regime or an institution.

11. "emptiness and": insert.

Chapter Fourteen: Problems of the Contemplative Life

1. Psalm 111:10.

2. "original" replaces a word blotted out.

3. The Little Brothers of Jesus is a congregation made up mostly of lay brothers. Inspired by the example of and writings of Charles de Foucauld (1858–1916), it was founded in Algeria in 1939 by a French priest, René Voillaume. The Little Brothers, living in small communities, seek to incorporate a contemplative spirituality into a simple lifestyle that involves a ministry of manual labor, especially among the poor.

4. "liberal": insert.

5. "today": insert.

6. "in 'togetherness'": insert.

7. "he" replaces "one" three times in these two sentences.

8. "Titian": insert. Venetian painter Titian (Tiziano Vecellio, 1490–1576) rates highly among the Renaissance artists. Among his many celebrated works is the *Assumption of the Virgin,* an altarpiece for a church in Venice.

9. "Praxiteles": insert. Praxiteles was a Greek sculptor of the fourth century B.C. whose few surviving works include *Hermes Carrying Dionysius.*

10. Jackson Pollock (1912–56), American painter and master of abstract expressionism, used abstract art to express rather than illustrate feelings.

11. Merton's footnote here reads: "The figure is based on experience and is exact."

12. "refuse to" replaces "will not."

13. "full" replaces "strict."

14. "liberation and relief" replaces "pleasure."

15. "manifest" replaces "have."
16. "Twenty-two was the outside limit": insert.
17. Merton makes an attempt at inclusive language by adding here "or woman." Regretfully, I have bracketed "or woman," as it does not fit with the personal pronominal adjectives that follow.
18. "the secular business which fills": insert.
19. "Sunday reminds us . . . properly oriented": insert.
20. "being" replaces "person."

Chapter Fifteen: Prospects and Conclusions

1. See Chapter 14, note 3.
2. Charles de Foucauld (1859–1916), whose writings inspired the founding of the Little Brothers of Jesus and also the Little Sisters of Jesus, spent several years in the military, and then abandoned the practice of faith for a while, only to return to it and become a Trappist monk. Later he left the Trappists to become a hermit in the Sahara desert.
3. The Tuaregs are nomadic tribes of the northern Sahara who have retained their own alphabet and a feudal system of living. They are fiercely independent people who resisted any colonial invasion of their land. They are mostly Muslim by religion.
4. " 'seculars' " replaces "laypeople."
5. The Hoggar (Ahagger) mountains in the central Sahara (in south Algeria) rise to more than 9,000 feet.
6. Jules Monchanin (1895–1957), a French priest, went to India and, together with another French priest, Henri de Saux (Abishiktananda), founded the Shantivanam ashram dedicated to the Holy Trinity.
7. "carefully preserved" replaces "kept."
8. " 'native' ": insert.
9. "an arbitrary" replaces "a corrupt."
10. See Chapter 10, note 8.
11. "what" replaces "the."
12. "that he seeks" replaces "to seek."

Appendix B: Tables of Contents: A Comparison

1. In both drafts (2 and 4) Merton numbered this chapter as well as the preceding one Chapter 4.
2. It is worth noting that pp. 1–56 are identical in drafts 2 and 4.
3. Merton mistakenly numbered this Chapter 7.
4. Pp. 57–77b have been added in draft 4. They have palimpsest numbers underneath, namely, 23–44. These palimpsest numbers suggest that this material came from some earlier material that I have not been able to identify. But clearly they existed in another document before their insertion into draft 4 (and, therefore, the presumption is that they existed before Merton made this summer rewrite of *What Is Contemplation?*).
5. This chapter and the next have no chapter numbers in drafts 2 and 4. Note that this chapter (now labeled 7; pp. 78–84) and the following chapter (now labeled 8; pp. 85–89) of draft 4 are identical with twelve pages (7 pages and 5 pages) in draft 2, but in draft 2 these pages are unnumbered.

6. Chapter 9 (pp. 90–94) has been added in draft 4. Except for three paragraphs (about a letter of St. John of the Cross), these pages are taken directly from *What Is Contemplation?*

7. Chapters 10–15 are pp. 53–108 in draft 2. These same chapters are pp. 95–150 in draft 4. Pp. 53–108 from draft 2 become in draft 4 the palimpsest numbers underneath pp. 95–150.

Since pp. 78–150 of draft 4 are pages that already exist in draft 2 (though with a different pagination), it was an easy matter to straighten out the mistake whereby draft 4 has two p. 77s. This was corrected in draft 3 (77b becoming 78 and 78 becoming 79, etc.). This means that draft 3 is one page longer in numbering than draft 4 and hence has 151 pages.

It may seem strange to say that draft 3 is a correction of draft 4. One would think it ought to be the other way around. My reason for this is that what I am designating as draft 4 is *the draft that Merton worked on last*. It is the draft on which Merton made the "corrections and additions" of 1968. I might also add that what I am calling draft 4 actually has no draft designation. What I am referring to as draft 3 is so designated in the draft at the Thomas Merton Center at Bellarmine University in Louisville, Kentucky (though it is my belief that these designations—draft 1, 2, 3—were made not by Merton, but by a curator of the Merton Center).

Index